SNACKS & GAMES

A Fun, Lesson-based Snack & Game for Each Lesson!

Noah's Park® Children's Church Snacks & Games Book (Green Edition)

Product Developer:	Karen Pickering
Managing Editor:	Doug Schmidt
Editor:	Judy Gillispie
Contributing Writers:	René Stewart
	Diane Cory
	Nancy Sutton
	Karen Schmidt
	Gail Rohlfing
Interior Design:	Mike Riester
Cover Design:	Todd Mock
Illustrations:	Chris Sharp

Published by Cook Communications Ministries
4050 Lee Vance View · Colorado Springs, CO 80918-7100
www.cookministries.com

Printed in Canada.

ISBN: 0-7814-3844-6   101796

TABLE OF CONTENTS

TABLE OF CONTENTS

TABLE OF CONTENTS

INTRODUCTION

The snacks and games provided in this book are coordinated with the lessons in the Noah's Park Leader's Guide. These pages are reproducible so that you can give each Park Patrol member or leader involved with snacks or games a copy for the individual lessons. You will notice that for each lesson the snack suggestion and elementary game are listed on one page and that the same snack suggestion and the preschool game are listed on the back of that page.

You may choose to keep all the children together during Snack Shack or you may separate the children into their age-appropriate groups before the snack. Use the method that works best for your situation. This may be determined by the number of children participating, by your room arrangement, or other factors.

When the children arrive for Children's Church the first week, take time to have the parents fill out a registration form. (Your Children's Ministry Director may have a form that is used for this purpose.) Be sure to have parents list any food allergies and keep this information in the classroom so that you can refer to it. Also be sure to have the parents indicate any physical limitations that might be affected by the games (such as asthma, etc.).

Basic supplies you should keep on hand for snacks:
· Napkins
· Cups
· Paper Plates
· Paper Towels
· Plastic spoons and forks
· Craft sticks to spread (instead of plastic knives)
· Crackers (for children who have allergies and cannot eat the day's snack suggestion)
· Sponges
· Disposable Wipes
· Dishpan and Soap
· Resealable plastic bags (to send snacks home that the children may not finish)

LESSON 1 SNACK:
Hidden Treats

Supplies: Bar cookies or granola bars with fruit filling · Napkins · Drink and cups

Directions: Give each child a cup of juice and a bar cookie. As they eat their snack, talk with them about what is hidden inside their cookies. **What a surprise! We didn't see what was inside until we bit into the cookie. We don't always know everything. But who does know even about hidden things? Jesus knows all about us.**

LESSON 1 ELEMENTARY GAME:
Getting to Know You

Supplies: Paper · Pencils · Container labeled "Jesus Knows" · Three to five chairs

Directions: Give each child a piece of paper and a pencil. Ask the kids to write their names along with two or three things about themselves that the others may not know about them. You might want to suggest things like hobbies, vacation places, or what they'd like to be when they grow up. Collect the papers and put them into the container labeled "Jesus Knows." Explain to the kids that Jesus already knows all the things they wrote down even if no one else does.

Depending on the size of your group, place three to five chairs in front for the "contestants" to sit on. The "audience" will sit on the floor. Read the clues given about one contestant and let the audience guess which child the clues describe. Have the Park Patrol members help you organize the contestants and clues so that the clues match one of the contestants sitting on the chairs. Allow each child to have a turn as a contestant.

LESSON 1 SNACK:
Hidden Treats

Supplies: Bar cookies or granola bars with fruit filling · Napkins · Drink and cups

Directions: Give each child a cup of juice and a bar cookie. As they eat their snack, talk with them about what is hidden inside their cookies. **What a surprise! We didn't see what was inside until we bit into the cookie. We don't always know everything. But who does know even about hidden things? Jesus knows all about us.**

LESSON 1 PRESCHOOL GAME:
Name Trade

Supplies: None

Directions: Have the children sit in a circle. Assign each child the name of one of Jesus' helpers: Philip, Nathanael, Andrew, or Peter. Use each name at least twice. Have the children practice saying their names so they remember which is theirs.

In our Bible story, Jesus knew all about Nathanael, because Jesus knows about all of us! Philip, Andrew, and Peter were Jesus' followers too. So let's play a game about them. When I call out your Bible name, trade places with the other person in our circle who has the same name. Call out the names, one at a time, using the following sentences:

> **Jesus knew Nathanael was reading God's Word.**
> **Jesus asked Philip to be His helper.**
> **One of Jesus' helpers was Andrew.**
> **Another of Jesus' helpers was Peter.**

It may take a little prompting to get kids to remember their names and switch places when their Bible character is called. You may repeat sentences or add other true ones for as long as you'd like. For more fun, tell the kids that when you call out "You are important to Jesus," all the children must switch places.

LESSON 2 SNACK:
Trail Mix

Supplies: Small paper cups · Trail mix (store-bought or home-made using any of these: raisins, dried fruit pieces, pretzels, fish crackers, cereal)

Directions: Mix ingredients in a large bowl or plastic bag. Scoop into paper cups and enjoy.

LESSON 2 ELEMENTARY GAME:
Packin' My Knapsack Relay

Supplies: Two backpacks · Two identical sets of various traveling items (comb, toothpaste, hand towel, coins, sandals, toy food)

Directions: Divide the children into two teams and have them line up for a relay race. Give each team an empty backpack. Place the traveling items opposite each team at the other end of your game area.

At your signal, the first child on each team puts on the backpack, runs to the pile of traveling items, places one item inside the backpack, zips it, and runs back to their team. They give the backpack to the next child, who repeats the process. The first team to fill their backpack wins.

You can add variety to the game by giving each child a different way to "travel"—running, skipping, walking backward, tip-toeing, and so on.

LESSON 2 SNACK:
Trail Mix

Supplies: Small paper cups · Trail mix (store-bought or home-made using any of these: raisins, dried fruit pieces, pretzels, fish crackers, cereal)

Directions: Mix ingredients in a large bowl or plastic bag. Scoop into paper cups and enjoy.

LESSON 2 PRESCHOOL GAME:
Ball Pass

Supplies: Two soft balls

Directions: Have the children sit in a circle with you. **In our Bible story, the man's son was very sick. The man traveled to another town to see Jesus. Pass this ball around the circle.** Pass one of the balls to your right. Have the children keep passing the ball as you talk. **The man found Jesus in the town. Pass this ball around the circle the other way until the balls meet.** Pass the other ball to your left. When the balls meet, get both of the balls from that child. **What did Jesus tell the man?** (Go home. His son would be well.) **The man hurried home.** Again pass one of the balls to your right. **His servants met him on the way.** Again pass the other ball to your left. **They told him his son was better. The man and his servants hurried home. Pass the balls as quickly as you can around the circle.**

LESSON 3 SNACK:
Funny Faces

Supplies: Round crackers · Mini carrots · Thinly sliced apple wedges · Orange slices · Raisins · Paper plates

Directions: On each plate place two round crackers, one carrot, two apple wedges, two orange slices, and two raisins. Tell the children to make a face on their plate by using the food you have given them. They may use the carrot for the nose, crackers with raisins on top for eyes, apple wedges for the mouth and orange slices for ears. Or the kids may come up with their own creative face. After they assemble their food face, talk about how important eyes are.

LESSON 3 ELEMENTARY GAME:
Obstacle Course

Supplies: Blindfold for each child · Obstacles (chairs, tables, laundry baskets, ropes, hula hoops, etc.)

Directions: Build an obstacle course in your game area. Provide spaces for the kids to climb over, crawl under, or go around obstacles while following a path. Consider using supplies such as chairs, tables, laundry baskets, ropes, hula hoops, and so on. The course may also include stations that say "jump in the air five times" or "touch your index fingers together above your head" or "turn in a circle two times."

Blindfold one child at a time and let them begin the course, with only verbal directions from you or a Park Patrol member to start off. (Have an adult close by to provide a safe situation.) When the child begins to get confused, send in a Park Patrol member to take the child's hand and guide him or her through the course.

When finished, briefly discuss with the kids how good it feels to have help to walk on a hard path and how Jesus is with us, even when we can't see Him.

LESSON 3 SNACK:
Funny Faces

Supplies: Round crackers · Mini carrots · Thinly sliced apple wedges
· Orange slices · Raisins · Paper plates

Directions: On each plate place two round crackers, one carrot,
two apple wedges, two orange slices, and two raisins. Tell the children
to make a face on their plate by using the food you have given them.
They may use the carrot for the nose, crackers with raisins on top for
eyes, apple wedges for the mouth and orange slices for ears. Or the
kids may come up with their own creative face. After they assemble
their food face, talk about how important eyes are.

LESSON 3 PRESCHOOL GAME:
Blind Trust Game

Supplies: Masking tape · Optional: blindfolds

Directions: Use masking tape to make a simple, winding path across
the floor. Be sure there aren't any obstacles nearby.

Divide the children into pairs. **In our Bible story, Jesus put mud
on a blind man's eyes and asked him to go to a special pool
to wash it off. Pretend one of you is the blind man. Keep
your eyes closed. The other one is your friend. Let your
friend lead you along the path to the pool. The blind man
needs to trust his friend to get him to the pool.**

Let the "friends" carefully lead the "blind men" along the path. At
the end of the path, have them switch places and walk back. Remind
the friend who can see to do a good job of not letting the "blind
friend" walk into anyone or anything.

LESSON 4 SNACK:
Donut Sheep

Supplies: Powdered sugar coated donut holes · Chocolate sprinkles for decoration · Small paper plates · Toothpicks

Directions: Give each child a plate and two donut holes, a toothpick, and some sprinkles. The children can use one donut for the head and another for the body of a sheep. The toothpicks can be used to connect them together. Use the chocolate sprinkles for eyes, nose, and mouth. (The sprinkles may need to be gently pressed into the donut to stay in place.)

LESSON 4 ELEMENTARY GAME:
Sheep Seek

Supplies: Assorted small sheep: toys, stuffed animals, pictures, etc.

Directions: Divide the class in two groups. The first group hides the sheep in the area that you designate. Set clear boundaries so the children know where to hide the sheep. The second group waits in a different area until the sheep are all hidden. Group 2 looks for the sheep while Group 1 watches. Group 1 may give clues by saying "baa" when someone from Group 2 walks near a hidden sheep. When all the sheep have been found, switch groups to give the "hiders" a chance to be the "seekers."

LESSON 4 SNACK:
Donut Sheep

Supplies: Powdered sugar coated donut holes · Chocolate sprinkles for decoration · Small paper plates · Toothpicks

Directions: Give each child a plate and two donut holes, a toothpick, and some sprinkles. The children can use one donut for the head and another for the body of a sheep. The toothpicks can be used to connect them together. Use the chocolate sprinkles for eyes, nose, and mouth. (The sprinkles may need to be gently pressed into the donut to stay in place.)

LESSON 4 PRESCHOOL GAME:
Shepherd Game

Supplies: Chairs, large blocks, etc.

Directions: Make a "sheep pen" by building a circle out of chairs, large blocks, or any other classroom items. Leave an opening on one side to serve as a doorway. You could use the same circle that was used for the Preschool Bible Story.

Choose one child to be the shepherd. The others are the sheep. **In our Bible story, Jesus told us about the Good Shepherd. A shepherd takes care of his sheep. The sheep will be outside the pen. When the shepherd calls the sheep by name, the sheep runs to the sheep pen.** (If the shepherd doesn't remember a child's name, be ready to help tell the name.)

If you have older preschoolers, you could choose one child to be a wolf. The wolf could tag a sheep who is outside of the pen. The sheep would then be "frozen." The shepherd would have to bring that sheep inside the pen to "unfreeze" him or her.

LESSON 5 SNACK:
Fish and Seawater

Supplies: Fish and sea-animal-shaped crackers · A blue or green beverage · Napkins · Cups

Directions: Give the children crackers shaped like sea animals or fish on a napkin. Serve them a blue or green drink to represent water. The children might enjoy identifying the different types of sea animals on their napkins.

LESSON 5 ELEMENTARY GAME:
Stormin' at Sea

Supplies: None

Directions: Explain to the kids that your class will "make a storm." You will give commands to lead the children through the stages of a storm. Have the children stand in a circle so they can see the "storm" as it grows. Make a rule that the children may not bump into each other or leave their spots during the "storm." After each command, pause for several seconds to let the children do the action. Start quietly and make the storm grow louder, using commands something like this:

Gently sway your hands in the breeze. Blow air quietly through your mouth. Rock back and forth as if you're a wave. Make a quiet thunder sound, rumbling far away. Show bigger waves rolling in with your hands. Clap your hands to show a flash of lightning. Rock back and forth harder. Make the thunder boom loudly. When the storm is as loud and long as you would like, say, **Jesus says, "Quiet! Be Still!"** Direct the children to immediately return to soft swaying and say, **"Shhhh."**

LESSON 5 SNACK:
Fish and Seawater

Supplies: Fish and sea-animal-shaped crackers · A blue or green beverage · Napkins · Cups

Directions: Give the children crackers shaped like sea animals or fish on a napkin. Serve them a blue or green drink to represent water. The children might enjoy identifying the different types of sea animals on their napkins.

LESSON 5 PRESCHOOL GAME:
Boat on the Lake

Supplies: None

Directions: Divide the children into pairs. If you have an odd number of students, be part of a pair yourself or have a Park Patrol helper join your group. Have the children sit on the floor facing each other with legs extended. It's fine if knees are bent as long as the bottoms of feet are touching. They make a boat by holding each other's hands.

Can you row your boat out into the sea? Encourage children to bend forward and backward while holding each other's hands. **Can you feel the wind and rain?** Have the children rock from side to side, still holding hands. **Can you feel the waves?** The children lift their arms up and down, from one side to the other. **Jesus told the wind and rain to be still.** Have the children freeze. Repeat with different partners as time allows.

LESSON 6 SNACK:
Man on a Mat

Supplies: Rectangular crackers · Baby carrots · String cheese, sliced like a flat circle · Small plates

Directions: Have the children make the man on the mat from the Bible story. They use the cracker for the mat, the circle of cheese for the head, and the carrot for the body. Many children do not like food mixed together, so if they would rather eat their snack pieces separately, allow them to do so. (Be aware of children with dairy allergies.)

LESSON 6 ELEMENTARY GAME:
Blanket Teamwork Challenge

Supplies: A blanket per group

Directions: Divide the children into groups of about seven with a Park Patrol helper in each. Give each group a blanket. Designate one area in the room as the pool of Bethesda and another place where the children are to start. Have the children work within their groups to get "a sick man" to the pool of Bethesda. They do this by having one small child be the "sick man" and get on the blanket. The others must brainstorm a way to effectively and safely get the "sick man" on his blanket to the pool. The "sick man" may help brainstorm but may not help with the moving effort. Be sure the children know that this is not a race, but a challenge to see which group can think of a creative way to safely transport their "sick man" to the pool. (Be sure an adult supervises this activity. You may want to discourage the children from carrying the "sick man." There are alternatives such as pulling him on the blanket on the floor or having him supported under his arms by two helpers, etc.)

LESSON 6 SNACK:
Man on a Mat

Supplies: Rectangular crackers · Baby carrots · String cheese, sliced like a flat circle · Small plates

Directions: Have the children make the man on the mat from the Bible story. They use the cracker for the mat, the circle of cheese for the head, and the carrot for the body. Many children do not like food mixed together, so if they would rather eat their snack pieces separately, allow them to do so. (Be aware of children with dairy allergies.)

LESSON 6 PRESCHOOL GAME:
Pick Up Your Mat and Come

Supplies: Towel or piece of paper for each child

Directions: Give each child a towel, and have the children line up across one side of the room, lying down on their towels. Choose one child to be the leader and stand at the opposite end of the room. The leader says, **"Pick up your mat and ___,"** filling in the blank with one way to move, such as walking, hopping, skipping, walking backward, and so on. The children should stand up, pick up their towels, and move to the leader in the way named. After each round, choose a new leader and have the children return to their original spots with their towels.

LESSON 7 SNACK:
Snack Service

Supplies: Serving bowls and serving spoons · Small finger-foods that can each go in its own bowl (raisins, nuts, fish crackers, small candies, etc.) · Pitcher of water · Plates or napkins · Paper cups

Directions: Place each snack in its own bowl. Let the children practice "serving in love" by wiping off the table, setting out the snack supplies, and making sure there are enough chairs. Encourage the children to "serve" one another the snack bowls and water. (Be sure to find out if any children have food allergies, especially nuts or chocolate, and make sure they do not touch any of those treats.)

LESSON 7 ELEMENTARY GAME:
Follow the Leader

Supplies: None

Directions: Jesus set an example for us to follow. Lead the children in a game of "Follow the Leader." In addition to the usual actions (jumping, hopping, skipping, tiptoeing, giant steps, etc.), include actions that remind the children of God's love. You might have the children pretend to wash each other's feet, give each other a hug, or shake hands. Also stop periodically to pass a loving message down the line, such as "You're a great friend." or "You are special." or "God loves you."

LESSON 7 SNACK:
Snack Service

Supplies: Serving bowls and serving spoons · Small finger-foods that can each go in its own bowl (raisins, nuts, fish crackers, small candies, etc.) · Pitcher of water · Plates or napkins · Paper cups

Directions: Place each snack in its own bowl. Let the children practice "serving in love" by wiping off the table, setting out the snack supplies, and making sure there are enough chairs. Encourage the children to "serve" one another the snack bowls and water. (Be sure to find out if any children have food allergies, especially nuts or chocolate, and make sure they do not touch any of those treats.)

LESSON 7 PRESCHOOL GAME:
Heart Hide and Seek

Supplies: Red construction paper, scissors

Preparation: Cut out five small paper hearts for each child. Hide the hearts around your room.

Directions: Explain to the children that paper hearts are hidden in the room and that each child should look for five. You may need to give clues for children who need help.

After all the hearts have been found, encourage the children to give their paper hearts to family members and friends throughout the week. Remind them that they can show love to others, just as Jesus showed love to His friends.

LESSON 8 SNACK:
Happy Face Cookies

Supplies: Round sugar cookies · Icing in a squeeze tube · Plates · Napkins

Directions: Give each child a plate, napkin, and cookie. Let the children take turns squeezing icing to make a happy face on their cookie. They may not want to stop squeezing when they have two eyes and a smile! Be specific on what they can do and then keep a watchful eye.

LESSON 8 ELEMENTARY GAME:
Forgiven Tag

Supplies: None

Directions: Forgiven tag is much like freeze tag. One person (or more if you have a large group) chases the rest of the children. When the tagger touches someone, he says, "You have done wrong." The tagged person kneels on the floor and waits until all the other children have been tagged. Then the tagger returns to each child, touches him, and says, "God forgives you." When everyone has been forgiven, a new game starts with a new tagger.

LESSON 8 SNACK:
Happy Face Cookies

Supplies: Round sugar cookies · Icing in a squeeze tube · Plates · Napkins

Directions: Give each child a plate, napkin, and cookie. Let the children take turns squeezing icing to make a happy face on their cookie. They may not want to stop squeezing when they have two eyes and a smile! Be specific on what they can do and then keep a watchful eye.

LESSON 8 PRESCHOOL GAME:
Love Bridge

Supplies: None

Directions: This game is a version of the familiar children's game "London Bridge." Choose two children to be the bridge. These children face each other holding both of their partner's hands. They then raise their clasped hands to create the bridge. The rest of the children walk in a line under the bridge and circling back around again for more turns. As they walk, sing these words to the tune of "London Bridge:"

> **Jesus shows us God forgives,**
>
> **God forgives, God forgives.**
>
> **Jesus shows us God forgives.**
>
> **God loves** (child's name).

The children fill in the blank by singing the name of the child who is under the bridge at that moment. The two children forming the bridge drop their hands to catch that child. That child and a friend of his choosing become the new bridge for another round.

LESSON 9 SNACK:
Sharing Mix

Supplies: Small paper cups · Peanuts · Raisins · Miniature pretzels · Dried banana slices · Jellybeans

Directions: Let the children choose from among the ingredients you have supplied to create their own trail mix. Encourage the children to show kindness to one another by sharing and taking turns.

LESSON 9 ELEMENTARY GAME:
Kindness Drill

Supplies: One beanbag per child

Directions: Give each child a beanbag to balance on his or her head. They may not hold it on. Have the children walk freely around the room. If the beanbag falls, the child who dropped it may not pick it up; he must stand still until another child helps him. Other children may risk losing their own beanbags to pick up the dropped beanbag and place it back on the child's head. Continue the game for several minutes. Afterward, ask the children how many others they were able to show kindness to by helping them.

LESSON 9 SNACK:
Sharing Mix

Supplies: Small paper cups · Peanuts · Raisins · Miniature pretzels · Dried banana slices · Jellybeans

Directions: Let the children choose from among the ingredients you have supplied to create their own trail mix. Encourage the children to show kindness to one another by sharing and taking turns.

LESSON 9 PRESCHOOL GAME:
Rock, Rock, Sand

Supplies: None

Directions: Have the children sit in a circle for this variation of "Duck, Duck, Goose." This game reinforces the Preschool Bible Story.

Choose one child to be the builder. The builder walks around the outside of the circle, tapping each child on the shoulder while saying, "rock." When the builder taps a child on the shoulder and says, "sand," that child gets up and chases the builder around the circle.

The last child back to the open spot becomes the new builder. Encourage each builder to say one thing he or she knows about God before continuing the game.

LESSON 10 SNACK:
Apple Stars and Dip

Supplies: Apples · Sharp knife · Fruit dip (peanut butter, yogurt, caramel, etc.) · Plates · Napkins

Directions: Cut the apples crossways so the core shows. The seeds will form a star shape. Point this out before further slicing the apples for the children to dip and eat. (If you choose a peanut butter dip, provide an alternative for children with nut allergies. Also be aware of children with dairy allergies.)

LESSON 10 ELEMENTARY GAME:
Day and Night

Supplies: Two signs · Masking tape

Preparation: Make two signs labeled "DAY" and "NIGHT."

Directions: Hang the "DAY" sign at one end of the room and the "NIGHT" sign at the other. Have the children stand by you in the center of the room. Call out activities that we do during the day or night. After you call each activity, the children run to the side of the room that best fits when they do that activity. Some activities may be done at either time so the children will run in different directions.

Some suggested activities to call are: **Go to church. Go to school. Take a bath. Swing on the swing set. Watch TV. Go to sleep. Pray. Spend time with Dad. Make dinner with Mom. Listen to a Bible story. Play ball.**

Remind the children to be careful as they run so no one gets hurt.

LESSON 10 SNACK:
Apple Stars and Dip

Supplies: Apples · Sharp knife · Fruit dip (peanut butter, yogurt, caramel, etc.) · Plates · Napkins

Directions: Cut the apples crossways so the core shows. The seeds will form a star shape. Point this out before further slicing the apples for the children to dip and eat. (If you choose a peanut butter dip, provide an alternative for children with nut allergies. Also be aware of children with dairy allergies.)

LESSON 10 PRESCHOOL GAME:
Sun and Moon Tag

Supplies: None

Directions: You or a Park Patrol helper will be "IT." It tries to tag children and call either "day" or "night." The tagged child must respond by saying either "sun" (for day) or "moon" (for night). If the tagged child says the correct word, he or she is free. If the answer is incorrect, the child has to stand still until "freed" (tagged) by another player.

LESSON 11 SNACK:
Sky, Water, and Land

Supplies: Blue gelatin · Miniature marshmallows · Graham crackers
· Small plates · Spoons

Directions: Allow the children to create their own pictures of the
Bible story before eating them. Give each child a plate, along with a
scoop of blue gelatin for water, miniature marshmallows for clouds
(representing the sky), and graham crackers for land.

LESSON 11 ELEMENTARY GAME:
Sky, Water, and Land Relay

Supplies: Pictures of animals, birds, fish, and different kinds of land,
water, and sky · Tape · Paper and marker

Preparation: Make three signs labeled "SKY," "WATER," and "LAND."
Draw a little picture to represent what each sign says (for nonreaders).
Find at least two pictures for each child showing animals, birds, fish, and
different kinds of land, water, and sky.

Directions: Hang the signs on a wall (or place them on the floor or a
table), a few feet apart from each other. At the opposite end of the
room, designate a starting line. Line up teams of four or five at the
starting line for a relay.

Place all the pictures in a pile, upside down, at the starting point of
each team. Have a Park Patrol helper with tape waiting by each sign.

At your signal, the first person on each team picks up a picture, decides
if it belongs with the water, sky, or land group, and races to that sign.
Park Patrol helpers should help them tape it under that sign. The
player races back to their team and tags the second person to repeat
the process. The first team to have all their pictures correctly in place
wins.

Children should hang pictures of fish by the "WATER" sign, birds by the
"AIR" sign, and animals by the "LAND" sign.

LESSON 11 SNACK:
Sky, Water, and Land

Supplies: Blue gelatin · Miniature marshmallows · Graham crackers · Small plates · Spoons

Directions: Allow the children to create their own pictures of the Bible story before eating them. Give each child a plate, along with a scoop of blue gelatin for water, miniature marshmallows for clouds (representing the sky), and graham crackers for land.

LESSON 11 PRESCHOOL GAME:
Skip to the Sky, Land, and Ocean

Supplies: Three pictures: sky, a mountain, and water · Masking tape

Preparation: Tape each picture in a different area of the room.

Directions: Gather the children into the center of the room. **God made the world. He made many wonderful things. He made the sky.** Point to the sky picture. **He made the oceans.** Point to the ocean picture. **He made the land.** Point to the mountain picture.

Skip to the sky that God made. The children should skip to the sky picture and back. **Hop to the ocean that God made.** The children should run to the ocean picture and back. **Run to the land that God made.** The children should run to the mountain picture and back.

Continue the game with the children suggesting different actions.

LESSON 12 SNACK:
Food Fair

Supplies: Seasonal foods (see suggestions below) · Plates · Cups · Napkins

Directions: Bring in a food item that represents each season, such as:
Winter: hot chocolate, fresh-baked cookies (warmed up to feel fresh out of the oven)
Spring: hot cross buns, gummy worms
Summer: watermelon, popsicles
Fall: apple pie, pumpkin bread, hot apple cider

As they eat, discuss with the children the variety of foods we enjoy because God made different seasons.

LESSON 12 ELEMENTARY GAME:
Four Seasons

Supplies: Paper · Marker · Masking tape

Preparation: Make four signs: "Summer," "Winter," "Spring," "Fall." Tape one sign up in each of the four corners of your room.

Directions: Have all the children begin in the center of the room. One person, called the Counter, stands in the middle of the room and counts to 10 with eyes closed. The rest of the children choose one corner to silently move to. With eyes still closed, the Counter names one season. The children standing in that corner must move back to the center and be seated. They are out for the rest of this round. The Counter closes eyes and counts again while the remaining children move to other corners. There must be at least one child in every corner. The Counter calls a season and the children in that corner are out. Continue until there is only one child left. That child is the new Counter for the next round.

LESSON 12 SNACK:
Food Fair

Supplies: Seasonal foods (see suggestions below) · Plates · Cups · Napkins

Directions: Bring in a food item that represents each season, such as:

Winter: hot chocolate, fresh-baked cookies (warmed up to feel fresh out of the oven)

Spring: hot cross buns, gummy worms

Summer: watermelon, popsicles

Fall: apple pie, pumpkin bread, hot apple cider

As they eat, discuss with the children the variety of foods we enjoy because God made different seasons.

LESSON 12 PRESCHOOL GAME:
Seasons Relay Game

Supplies: Ponder the Frog puppet · Clothing for each season (For example, raincoat for spring, sun hat and sunglasses for summer, oversized sweatshirt for fall, scarf and mittens for winter.)

Directions: Lay the clothing out in four separate piles, one for each season. Have the children stand at the opposite end of your game area. Name the season with the children as you hold up the clothing you brought for it.

Put on the Ponder puppet. **God made the seasons. When it's your turn, Ponder will call out a season. Run to the clothes for that season, put them on, and then take them off again. Run back to your group.** Make Ponder call out **"God made** (name a season)**"** for each child. The child runs the relay as described above.

Play until each child has had a turn. If you have a large group, you may want to have two sets of items for the children to use.

LESSON 13 SNACK:
Ants on a Log

Supplies: Celery sticks · Peanut butter or cream cheese · Raisins or peanuts · Plastic knives · Napkins

Directions: Show the children how to spread peanut butter or cream cheese in the hollow part of a celery stick to make a "log." Then they add a few raisins or peanuts for "ants."

(Find out if any children have allergies to milk products or nuts, and be sure they don't eat or touch those food items.)

LESSON 13 ELEMENTARY GAME:
Animal Acts

Supplies: List of animals

Preparation: Prior to class make a list of eight to ten animals that have distinctive characteristics and can be acted out. Some ideas are elephants, monkeys, ducks, dragonflies, and frogs. For added fun, find a fun fact to go along with each animal. (For example, a giraffe's tongue is six inches long; a hippopotamus can stay under water over five minutes; panda bears are only five inches long when they are born; the monarch butterfly flies thousands of miles every year.)

Directions: Have the children stand in a large circle. Explain that you will call out an animal for them to act out. They can move around the circle, making motions and sounds like the animal. Encourage the kids to enjoy watching each other as they imitate the animals. Allow about 30 seconds for each animal act. If you have fun facts, tell the kids one after each animal act. (This will give them a breather as they listen.)

LESSON 13 SNACK:
Ants on a Log

Supplies: Celery sticks · Peanut butter or cream cheese · Raisins or peanuts · Plastic knives · Napkins

Directions: Show the children how to spread peanut butter or cream cheese in the hollow part of a celery stick to make a "log." Then they add a few raisins or peanuts for "ants."

(Find out if any children have allergies to milk products or nuts, and be sure they don't eat or touch those food items.)

LESSON 13 PRESCHOOL GAME:
Animal Keeper

Supplies: None

Directions: Choose a child to be the animal keeper. Have the children sit in a circle. The animal keeper sits in the middle. The animal keeper says, "I take care of animals. What animal am I acting out?" The animal keeper then acts out an animal with motions and sounds. The child who correctly guesses the animal becomes the new animal keeper. Encourage children to raise their hands to guess the animal.

Play continues until all the children have had a turn being the animal keeper. You may need to whisper animal suggestions to the animal keeper. Remind the children that they may choose wild animals, farm animals, pets, birds, fish, insects, and reptiles.

LESSON 14 SNACK:
Picnic Snack

Supplies: Large tablecloth, blanket, or sheet · Large-sized animal crackers · Soft cream cheese · Sprinkles or other small toppings · Small plastic knives · Napkins · Small plates

Directions: Have a Noah's Park picnic. Allow the children to plan and make their own animal cracker creations.

Spread the tablecloth on the floor. Set up at least two stations at tables where the children can make their snacks. At these stations provide the cream cheese, toppings, knives, napkins, and plates. Direct the kids to spread the cream cheese on their animal cookie, then add toppings you have provided. (Be aware of dairy allergies.)

LESSON 14 ELEMENTARY GAME:
Grab the Coconut

Supplies: A ball or a real coconut · Masking tape

Preparation: Make a very large circle on the floor with masking tape.

Directions: Why do you think we have rules? *(Children may say: rules are for safety, for fairness, to make games easier to play, to make sure everyone has fun and gets a chance to play, and so on.)* Then briefly discuss how rules are part of God's plan for us. God gives us rules in the Bible because He cares about us.

Divide the children into two or three teams, depending on your group size. Assign one child on each team the name of a Noah's Park animal (Honk the Camel, Shadow the Raccoon, Ponder the Frog, Stretch the Giraffe, Dreamer the Rhinoceros, Screech the Monkey, Howler the Lion, Ivory the Elephant, and Flutter the Dove). If you have more children than animals, make more teams or rotate the children in and out of the game.

Have the children stand around the masking tape circle. They are not allowed to step on or inside the circle unless their animal is called. Place a ball or coconut in the center. When you call out an animal character, the children assigned that character run to the center to grab the coconut and run back outside the circle before being tagged by the other player. If both children should grab the coconut at the same time, have them return to their place and call out another name.

LESSON 14 SNACK:
Picnic Snack

Supplies: Large tablecloth, blanket, or sheet · Large-sized animal crackers · Soft cream cheese · Sprinkles or other small toppings · Small plastic knives · Napkins · Small plates

Directions: Have a Noah's Park picnic. Allow the children to plan and make their own animal cracker creations.

Spread the tablecloth on the floor. Set up at least two stations at tables where the children can make their snacks. At these stations provide the cream cheese, toppings, knives, napkins, and plates. Direct the kids to spread the cream cheese on their animal cookie, then add toppings you have provided. (Be aware of dairy allergies.)

LESSON 14 PRESCHOOL GAME:
Angel, May I?

Supplies: Optional: garland for halo

Directions: Choose one child to be the angel. The child could wear a garland halo. Have the angel stand at one end of the room. The other children line up at the opposite end of the room.

The angel calls out different commands, such as, "Take three giant steps." The children need to respond, "Angel, may I?" before they move the stated number of steps. If a child moves without asking, "Angel, may I?" he or she returns to the starting point. The first child to reach the angel needs to say, "God sent His Son, Jesus," before becoming the new angel.

LESSON 15 SNACK:
Bedtime Snack

Supplies: Graham crackers · Mini marshmallows · Napkins
· Optional: milk and cups

Directions: Give each child a whole graham cracker and four mini-marshmallows. Have the children break their graham crackers into four pieces along the lines. Tell the kids that the cracker is like Joseph's bed and the marshmallow is his pillow (each child will have have four "beds" and four "pillows"). As the children eat, let volunteers tell what happened in the Bible story.

LESSON 15 ELEMENTARY GAME:
Pillow Commands

Supplies: One or two bed pillows

Directions: Direct the children to sit in a large circle. If you have a large class, divide the children into two groups and make two circles. Place a bed pillow in the center of the circle. Explain that you are going to give directions and that the kids need to listen and obey. Have the children be seated attentively in between directions.

Commands that you give may include: **If you're wearing white shoes, come walk around the pillow two times. If you're wearing pants, come hop once over the pillow without touching it. If you have brown hair, walk around the outside of our circle once. If you're wearing a skirt, come pat the pillow three times. If you missed Sunday school last week, kneel next to the pillow with your head on your hands and pretend to sleep.** Add your own directions tailored to your class.

LESSON 15 SNACK:
Bedtime Snack

Supplies: Graham crackers · Mini marshmallows · Napkins
· Optional: milk and cups

Directions: Give each child a whole graham cracker and four mini-marshmallows. Have the children break their graham crackers into four pieces along the lines. Tell the kids that the cracker is like Joseph's bed and the marshmallow is his pillow (each child will have four "beds" and four "pillows"). As the children eat, let volunteers tell what happened in the Bible story.

LESSON 15 PRESCHOOL GAME:
Angel, Angel, Joseph

Supplies: None

Directions: This game is a variation of "Duck, Duck, Goose." Ask the children to sit in a circle. Choose one child to be the Runner. The child who is the Runner walks around the outside of the circle and taps the seated children on the shoulder while walking by. With each tap, the Runner says, "angel." But when the Runner taps a child and says, "Joseph," the Runner takes off running and the tagged child jumps up and chases the Runner. The Runner tries to make it to the tagged child's open spot before being tagged. If the Runner succeeds, the tagged child becomes the new Runner. But if the Runner gets tagged while being chased, the same child remains the Runner.

LESSON 16 SNACK:
Manger Snacks

Supplies: Butter-type crackers · Squeeze cheese · Pretzels sticks · Shredded cheese

Directions: Have the children make "mangers" with their snack ingredients: Spread squeeze cheese onto a full-sized butter-type cracker. Lay pretzels sticks on the cheese along the four sides to outline a manger. Sprinkle shredded cheese in the middle for hay. (Be aware of dairy allergies.)

LESSON 16 ELEMENTARY GAME:
Welcome Me Tag

Supplies: None

Directions: This game is played by everyone trying to give others a "welcome tag" while avoiding being tagged themselves. This is a walking, not a running, tag game. Remind the children to give gentle taps when tagging. This is also an "honesty" game, where each child keeps count for themselves.

Have the kids spread out in your playing area. At your signal, everyone tries to give a welcome by tagging as many other players as possible. The tagging is done by giving a pat on the upper back or shoulder. Tags on any other part of the body don't count. At the same time, players must avoid being tagged. It's okay to welcome the same player more than once, but a different player must be tagged in between. Players must keep count of the number of welcome tags they are able to give. At the end of one minute, stop the game. The player with the highest number of welcomes wins the game. If time permits, play the game again.

LESSON 16 SNACK:
Manger Snacks

Supplies: Butter-type crackers · Squeeze cheese · Pretzels sticks · Shredded cheese

Directions: Have the children make "mangers" with their snack ingredients: Spread squeeze cheese onto a full-sized butter-type cracker. Lay pretzels sticks on the cheese along the four sides to outline a manger. Sprinkle shredded cheese in the middle for hay. (Be aware of dairy allergies.)

LESSON 16 PRESCHOOL GAME:
Going to Bethlehem

Supplies: Rhythm sticks or a hand drum

Directions: Have the children pretend they are traveling to Bethlehem with Mary and Joseph. Say each line below, and have the children repeat it after you. Use rhythm sticks or a hand drum to create a beat. For each line, change the speed or the rhythm. Suggestions are given below. The children may clap along on the beats. For a more active game, have the children stand in place or walk in a circle, imitating the beats you make. You could also let the children add other details to the story to extend the game.

We're traveling to Bethlehem. (moderate speed)

Here's a steep hill that we have to climb. (slowly)

We're almost there! I can see Bethlehem. (quickly)

We are very tired. We need a place to rest. (very slowly)

Jesus is born! Jesus is born! (quickly)

LESSON 17 SNACK:
Apples Stars

Supplies: Apples · Sharp knife · Plastic knives · Fruit-flavored cream cheese or soft caramel dip · Optional: cutting board

Directions: Slice an apple in half. Show the children how the seeds are arranged in a star shape. Tell the children that an apple can remind them of the star that shown over Bethlehem when Jesus was born.

Cut the apples into slices and pass them out. Let the children spread fruit-flavored cream cheese or soft caramel dip on their apple wedges.

LESSON 17 ELEMENTARY GAME:
Tricky Truths

Supplies: Masking tape

Directions: Make a large circle on the floor with masking tape. Have the kids stand spread out in a circle around you. Stand in the center, and make statements from the Bible stories of Jesus' birth that are either true are not. If you make a statement that is true, the kids pretend to fly like an angel one time around the circle. If the statement is false, the kids stoop down in place.

Use the following statements to play the game or make up your own.

Bible Story Statements:
An angel told the shepherds some good news. *(true)*
Jesus was born in a rich king's palace. *(false)*
The angels praised God for Jesus' birth. *(true)*
The shepherds praised God for Jesus' birth. *(true)*
Mean King Herod praised God for Jesus' birth. *(false)*
The shepherds did not make the long walk to Bethlehem. *(false)*
The shepherds found Jesus lying in a manger. *(true)*
A shepherd's job was to take care of giraffes and hippos. *(false)*
The sky filled with angels singing of God's glory and peace. *(true)*
Joseph found a room at a nice hotel for Jesus to be born in. *(false)*

LESSON 17 SNACK:
Apples Stars

Supplies: Apples · Sharp knife · Plastic knives · Fruit-flavored cream cheese or soft caramel dip · Optional: cutting board

Directions: Slice an apple in half. Show the children how the seeds are arranged in a star shape. Tell the children that an apple can remind them of the star that shown over Bethlehem when Jesus was born.

Cut the apples into slices and pass them out. Let the children spread fruit-flavored cream cheese or soft caramel dip on their apple wedges.

LESSON 17 PRESCHOOL GAME:
Where's the Baby in Bethlehem?

Supplies: Stand-up figure of baby Jesus (*Craft Book*, page GC·40) or a figure of baby Jesus from a non-breakable nativity set

Directions: Hide the figure of baby Jesus in your game area. Ask the children to lie down on their backs. **Let's pretend that we are shepherds near Bethlehem. It's nighttime. Angels have just told us about God's Son, Jesus, being born! What should we do? Let's get up and look for baby Jesus!** Encourage the children to find the hidden figure. When the figure is found, have the child who found it hide it again. Continue playing as time allows.

LESSON 18 SNACK:
Star Sandwiches

Supplies: White bread · Cheese slices · Star-shaped cookie cutters

Directions: Allow the children to cut bread and cheese with star-shaped cookie cutters to make sandwiches.

LESSON 18 ELEMENTARY GAME:
The Wise Men's Race

Supplies: Two gift-wrapped boxes · Two bath towels · Yellow construction paper · Scissors

Preparation: Cut two large stars from the construction paper, or use stars made earlier.

Directions: Divide the kids into two teams, and have them line up. At the opposite end of your playing area, place the two stars, one across from each team. Give each team a towel and a gift-wrapped box. Have the first pair on each team hold the towel stretched out between them with the gift balanced on the towel.

Tell the teams that they will race in pairs to bring "gifts" to Jesus. At your signal, they run to the star, touch it, and run back (bringing the gift with them). If the gift falls, the pair must stop to pick it up again. When the first pair reaches their team again, they give the towel to the next pair in line, place the gift on it, and let them race. The first team to race everyone on their team to the star and back again is the winner.

LESSON 18 SNACK:
Star Sandwiches

Supplies: White bread · Cheese slices · Star-shaped cookie cutters

Directions: Allow the children to cut bread and cheese with star-shaped cookie cutters to make sandwiches.

LESSON 18 PRESCHOOL GAME:
Follow the Star

Supplies: One paper star · Optional: Noah's Park puppets

Directions: This is a version of "Follow the Leader." Have the children line up behind you. Hold the star high in one hand as you lead. Instruct the children to follow you and do what you do. Move around the room, doing movement such as hopping, marching, flapping arms, clapping hands above head, taking baby steps, and so on. Do each movement for about 10 seconds before changing to a new one.

You could let the Noah's Park puppets "play" along with you by letting the children take turns holding them and helping them do similar movements.

LESSON 19 SNACK:
Edible Portraits

Supplies: Large round or oval crackers · Squeeze cheese · Raisins
· Plates or napkins

Directions: Allow the children to make a snack "portrait" with crackers to remind them that God made them and knows them. They use a cracker as a face, squeeze cheese for hair, and raisins for eyes nose, and mouth.

LESSON 19 ELEMENTARY GAME:
Who's Missing?

Supplies: None

Directions: Select someone to be the first guesser. A Park Patrol helper takes that child out of the room. Have the class select one child to hide somewhere in the room. At your signal, the Park Patrol helper brings the guesser back in. The children in the room tell the guesser, **"God knows who's missing!"** Then the guesser must figure out who is hiding just by looking at the other children and remembering who was there. Set a time limit, such as one minute. You may also offer a few clues if the child needs help, such as, **"God knows that the missing child has brown hair"** or **"God knows that the missing child is wearing a dress."**

LESSON 19 SNACK:
Edible Portraits

Supplies: Large round or oval crackers · Squeeze cheese · Raisins
· Plates or napkins

Directions: Allow the children to make a snack "portrait" with crackers to remind them that God made them and knows them. They use a cracker as a face, squeeze cheese for hair, and raisins for eyes nose, and mouth.

LESSON 19 PRESCHOOL GAME:
Finger to Finger

Supplies: Ponder the Frog puppet

Directions: Divide the children into pairs. Wear the Ponder puppet, and explain the game: Ponder will call out an instruction, such as, "Finger to finger." The children in each pair should follow the instruction by touching each other's finger. Ponder's instructions will become more challenging as the children play. Use instructions such as hand to hand, back to back, knee to knee, and then harder ones such as elbow to knee or wrist to ankle.

LESSON 20 SNACK:
Snack Jobs

Supplies: Two or three different kinds of healthy crackers · Bananas · Grapes or berries · Sweetened, powered drink mix · Pitcher · Plastic knife · Serving bowls · Plates · Cups

Directions: Give each child a job during snack time. Children may slice bananas into chunks, wash grapes or berries, arrange fruit in serving bowls, prepare the drink mix with water, serve the food or drinks, wipe tables, throw away disposable trash, and wash non-disposable items.

LESSON 20 ELEMENTARY GAME:
God's Job Race

Supplies: Noah's Park CD and CD player

Directions: Divide the children into three or four groups and give each group an occupational name, such as doctors, firefighters, and so on. Assign a different corner of the game area as each group's place of work. When you play music from the Noah's Park CD, the children begin to walk around the game area. When you stop the music and shout, **"Go to your job!"** the children run to their designated corner. The group with all its members at their jobs first is the winner for that round. Play the game several times as time permits. A variation would be to name the groups after home chores, such as dishwashers, bed-makers, pet feeders, and so on.

LESSON 20 SNACK:
Snack Jobs

Supplies: Two or three different kinds of healthy crackers · Bananas · Grapes or berries · Sweetened, powered drink mix · Pitcher · Plastic knife · Serving bowls · Plates · Cups

Directions: Give each child a job during snack time. Children may slice bananas into chunks, wash grapes or berries, arrange fruit in serving bowls, prepare the drink mix with water, serve the food or drinks, wipe tables, throw away disposable trash, and wash non-disposable items.

LESSON 20 PRESCHOOL GAME:
God Made Us Musical Game

Supplies: None

Directions: Have the children stand in a circle. Let them sing and act out the following words to the tune of "Hokey Pokey."

Put your hand in,

Put your hand out,

Put your hand in,

And shake it all about.

Everybody God made can give a little shout.

God made us—you and me!

Repeat for foot, leg, arm, and head.

LESSON 21 SNACK:
Candy Varieties

Supplies: A variety of candies or cookies · Water or juice · Napkins · Cups

Directions: Let the children choose their favorite kind of candy or cookie and try to explain why they like that kind best. Point out that different children like different kinds of candies or cookies.

LESSON 21 ELEMENTARY GAME:
Shoe Pass

Supplies: Noah's Park CD and CD player

Directions: Have the children sit in a circle. Each child removes one shoe. Encourage the children to try to sit on their other shoe so it doesn't show. Then play music from the Noah's Park CD and have the children pass their shoes around the circle in time with the music. Randomly stop the music. The kids must look carefully at the shoe they are holding and try to guess which child it belongs to. Let about half the children guess for this first round. Then start the music again, and let the kids pass the remaining shoes. Again stop the music, and let the rest of the children try to figure out whose shoe is whose.

When the kids are reunited with their shoes, talk briefly about how every child has different size feet and likes different styles of shoes.

Play the game a second time, this time passing the shoes in the other direction. See how well the children can remember the shoes to match them up with their owners.

LESSON 21 SNACK:
Candy Varieties

Supplies: A variety of candies or cookies · Water or juice · Napkins · Cups

Directions: Let the children choose their favorite kind of candy or cookie and try to explain why they like that kind best. Point out that different children like different kinds of candies or cookies.

LESSON 21 PRESCHOOL GAME:
Silly Connections

Supplies: None

Directions: God made you, and God made you special. God made you with lots of parts! Let's play a silly game.

Have each child stand in an area where he or she won't be touching anyone. You will ask the children to point to two different body parts, then try to touch those two together. **Point to your nose. Point to your wrist. Touch your nose with your wrist.**

Continue in the same pattern using the following pairs: **Touch your elbow to your knee; touch your nose to your leg; touch your head to your leg.** Encourage the children to create their own silly connections.

LESSON 22 SNACK:
Pretzel Hugs

Supplies: Pretzels (traditional shape) · Chocolate syrup · Small bowls

Directions: Pour chocolate into several bowls, and let the children dip their pretzels in the chocolate. (Be aware of children who may have chocolate allergies.) As they eat, talk about how the pretzel shapes look like hearts or arms hugging.

LESSON 22 ELEMENTARY GAME:
Esau, May We Cross Your Bridge?

Supplies: Masking tape

Directions: Use masking tape to make two long parallel lines in your game area, about three feet apart. This is the bridge. Choose one child to be Esau and stand on the bridge (between the two lines). The rest of the children stand on one side of the bridge.

The children call in unison, **"Esau, Esau, may we cross your bridge?"** Esau responds by giving clues as to who may cross. For example, **"You may hop across my bridge if you are wearing blue."** All the children wearing blue hop across to the other side of the lines. Then the remaining children call again, **"Esau, Esau, may we cross your bridge?"** Esau chooses another clue, such as, **"You may jump across my bridge if you are wearing black."** Children wearing black jump across the bridge. Each time Esau names a different color and movement.

At any time, Esau may answer the question by shouting, **"I forgot how to get along!"** and he races to tag anyone who has already crossed the bridge. At the same time, those who have already crossed race back over to the first side of the bridge. All children on the first side of the bridge are "safe." The first child tagged becomes the new Esau.

LESSON 22 SNACK:
Pretzel Hugs

Supplies: Pretzels (traditional shape) · Chocolate syrup · Small bowls

Directions: Pour chocolate into several bowls, and let the children dip their pretzels in the chocolate. (Be aware of children who may have chocolate allergies.) As they eat, talk about how the pretzel shapes look like hearts or arms hugging.

LESSON 22 PRESCHOOL GAME:
Hug Team

Supplies: None

Directions: Jacob and Esau hugged when they saw each other. They showed that they would get along, just as God wanted them to.

Have the children form two lines. The first child in each line turns and hugs the child behind him or her. The children keep passing this hug down the line. Then have the children turn the other way so that the last person is first. Send the hug back up the line.

To extend the game, ask the children what else they can pass down the line to show that they get along. (For example, a handshake, a high-five, a wink, or an arm link.)

LESSON 23 SNACK:
Golden Snacks

Supplies: Any gold or yellow colored snack (potato chips, golden raisins, yellow apple slices, etc.) · Serving plate(s) · Napkins or plates

Directions: Explain that gold was one of the offerings that kings gave to God at the temple in Bible times. Invite the children to offer a golden snack (on a serving plate) to someone else before taking their own. As the children eat, you could talk about what colors our coins are.

LESSON 23 ELEMENTARY GAME:
Coin Toss

Supplies: Containers (buckets, bowls, wastebaskets, etc.) · Lots of real or toy coins · Optional: Masking tape

Directions: Divide the children into groups of four or five. Give each group a container and each child at least four or five coins. Make sure the groups have space away from each other. Instruct the groups to place their container on the floor, stand in a circle around it, and then take three giant steps back from it. The children in each group will end up in a wide circle around their container. You may want to put a short masking tape line where each child should stand to keep them from moving closer to their container as they play.

At your signal, the children begin tossing their coins at their team's container, trying to get all of their coins into it. Coins that miss may be picked up by another team member and thrown again. Remind the children to keep three giant steps back from their team's container whenever they toss. (They may move to pick up stray coins.) Set a time limit, such as 30 seconds. When time is up, have all the teams stop and count the number of coins that made it into their container.

LESSON 23 SNACK:
Golden Snacks

Supplies: Any gold or yellow colored snack (potato chips, golden raisins, yellow apple slices, etc.) · Serving plate(s) · Napkins or plates

Directions: Explain that gold was one of the offerings that kings gave to God at the temple in Bible times. Invite the children to offer a golden snack (on a serving plate) to someone else before taking their own. As the children eat, you could talk about what colors our coins are.

LESSON 23 PRESCHOOL GAME:
King, May I Bring My Offering?

Supplies: Paper crown · Play money · Box with a hole in the lid

Directions: Choose one child to be the king and wear the crown. The king stands at one end of the room next to the box. The other children stand in a line at the other end of the room. Give each child a piece of play money.

The king tells the children, by name, to take a certain number of steps to bring an offering. Each child needs to ask, **"King, may I?"** before moving. After the king says, **"Yes, you may,"** the child takes the steps. The first child to put his or her money in the box is the new king.

Encourage the king to name steps like giant steps, baby steps, and backward steps.

LESSON 24 SNACK:
Tortilla Scrolls

Supplies: Small, soft tortillas · Plastic knives · Flavored cream cheese or squirt cheese

Directions: Let the children spread cream cheese or squirt cheese on a tortilla and then roll it up like a scroll. (Be aware of dairy allergies.)

LESSON 24 ELEMENTARY GAME:
Listen for the Word

Supplies: None

Directions: Have the children stand along a wall at one end of the room. Call out a "fact" from the Bible story. If it's true, the children take two giant steps forward. If it's false, they stand still. If they move forward on a false statement, they must go back to the wall. Those who listen and remember most carefully will reach the opposite wall first.

Use true and false facts from the Bible story and other parts of the lesson, such as:

Ezra read God's Word to the people. *(true)*
Ezra dropped the scroll when he started to read. *(false)*
The people listened carefully to God's Word. *(true)*
The people prayed and gave offerings too. *(true)*
Listening to God's Word is not important. *(false)*
The people worshiped God by reading and listening to His Word. *(true)*
It's not important for us to learn from the Bible. *(false)*
Ezra stood on a platform so people could hear and see him better. *(true)*
Grown-ups listened to Ezra, but children did not. *(false)*
Our Bible story about Ezra was from the Book of Nehemiah. *(true)*

You might also include the memory verse, said both correctly and incorrectly.

LESSON 24 SNACK:
Tortilla Scrolls

Supplies: Small, soft tortillas · Plastic knives · Flavored cream cheese or squirt cheese

Directions: Let the children spread cream cheese or squirt cheese on a tortilla and then roll it up like a scroll. (Be aware of dairy allergies.)

LESSON 24 PRESCHOOL GAME:
Parachute Play

Supplies: Flat sheet or small parachute

Directions: Spread the sheet or parachute flat on the floor. Have the children sit around it, evenly spaced. When they hold onto the parachute or sheet, have them roll the edge a couple times before grasping it. This will give them a stronger hold.

The people came to hear Ezra read God's Word. Have the children stand and walk in a circle while holding the parachute or sheet. Ezra stood on a special stage while he read God's Word. Have the children hold the parachute or sheet high above their heads. The people stood below and listened. Have the children quickly bring the edges of the parachute or sheet down to the ground.

Repeat the three actions in different orders.

LESSON 25 SNACK:
Temple Blocks

Supplies: Snacks that stack like building blocks (wafer cookies, graham crackers, rectangular crackers) · A sticky food spread (cream cheese, icing, peanut butter, etc.) · Plastic knives · Plates · Napkins

Directions: Give each child four or five "building blocks" and access to a food spread to use as "glue." Let the children try to build a simple temple (four walls and a roof) with their snack before eating it. (Be aware of food allergies when using nut and dairy products.)

LESSON 25 ELEMENTARY GAME:
Prayer Hoops

Supplies: Five boxes, many small balls (plastic or soft foam balls, wadded up paper, etc.)

Preparation: Clearly label five boxes: "Sad," "Happy," "Mad," "Thankful," and "Worried." Draw a simple face by each word to represent it.

Directions: Spread the five labeled boxes out in a large circle. Have the children stand in the middle (with their backs to each other) with as many small balls as you have on hand. **We worship God by praying to Him. We show our trust in Him by talking with Him about everything. Read the labels on the five boxes. These are five examples of times when you can talk to God—when you're sad, happy, mad, thankful, or worried.**

Direct the kids to practice "shooting hoops" by trying to toss a ball in each box. They may need to take turns and share the balls, and some children will need to retrieve balls already tossed. Challenge the kids to see how far back from a box they can stand and still make a basket.

LESSON 25 SNACK:
Temple Blocks

Supplies: Snacks that stack like building blocks (wafer cookies, graham crackers, rectangular crackers) · A sticky food spread (cream cheese, icing, peanut butter, etc.) · Plastic knives · Plates · Napkins

Directions: Give each child four or five "building blocks" and access to a food spread to use as "glue." Let the children try to build a simple temple (four walls and a roof) with their snack before eating it. (Be aware of food allergies when using nut and dairy products.)

LESSON 25 PRESCHOOL GAME:
Come to the Temple

Supplies: Large blocks or boxes

Directions: First have the children help you build a wall at one end of your game area using large blocks or boxes. Then have the class stand at the opposite end of the room.

King Solomon built a temple where people could worship God. Many people traveled to the temple. Let's travel to the temple too.

Have the children take turns walking, skipping, hopping, or tip-toeing to the "temple" and back. Encourage the children to add different ways they can get to the temple.

LESSON 26 SNACK:
Musical Bites

Supplies: Stick pretzels (to represent flutes or clarinets) · Bugle or funnel-shaped chips (for trumpets) · Round crackers (for cymbals) · Any other snack that could look like an instrument · Plates or napkins

Directions: Let the children pretend to play the snack instruments as they eat. Let the children share about instruments (including rhythm instruments) they have had a chance to play.

LESSON 26 ELEMENTARY GAME:
Instrument Tag

Supplies: Two blindfolds

Directions: Have the children stand in a large circle and join hands. Choose two children to be the Musician and the Instrument. Blindfold them and have them stand in the circle. The Musician walks around in the circle trying to find and tag the Instrument. The Instrument tries to avoid being touched by the Musician. Whenever the Musician wants a clue for where the Instrument is, the Musician says, **"Play me a song!"** The Instrument must respond by making a sound like an instrument ("toot-a-toot" or "plink, plink," etc.) The Musician and Instrument must stay inside the circle at all times. When the Musician finally tags the Instrument, they remove their blindfolds and join the circle. Two new children become the new players. You might want to set a time limit, such as one minute, for the Musician to tag the Instrument.

LESSON 26 SNACK:
Musical Bites

Supplies: Stick pretzels (to represent flutes or clarinets) · Bugle or funnel-shaped chips (for trumpets) · Round crackers (for cymbals) · Any other snack that could look like an instrument · Plates or napkins

Directions: Let the children pretend to play the snack instruments as they eat. Let the children share about instruments (including rhythm instruments) they have had a chance to play.

LESSON 26 PRESCHOOL GAME:
Catch the Music Leader

Supplies: None

Directions: This game is similar to "Duck, Duck, Goose." Choose one child to be the music leader. The rest of the children sit in a circle. Have the music leader walk around the outside of the circle. The music leader taps each child and says the name of an instrument (trumpet, harp, tambourine). It's okay for the music leader to repeat instruments. But if the music leader says, **"Sing a song,"** that child jumps up and runs after the music leader. Both children run around the circle. The first one back to the empty spot sits down. The other child becomes the new music leader.

Continue playing until all the children have had a turn being the music leader.

LESSON 27 SNACK:
Energy Bars

Supplies: An energy or granola type bar or another "quick energy" snack, such as trail mix, raisins, or fruit slices

Directions: Gather the children to the snack area. Have the Park Patrol pass out snacks to the children. If using some type of energy bars, you may want to divide them in half or into fourths. As the children eat the snack remind them that a snack that gives them power can remind them that Jesus is all-powerful.

LESSON 27 ELEMENTARY GAME:
Lazarus Relay

Supplies: Rolls of toilet tissue (one per team) or crepe paper streamer

Directions: Divide the class into teams of four or five. (If you have a small group, each team could have as few as three children.) Have each team select one individual to be "Lazarus." The rest of the team will be reponsible for wrapping and unwrapping Lazarus. Be sure to spread the teams out so they have sufficient room to work.

When you give the signal, have all the teams begin wrapping. (The person's mouth and nose should be left uncovered.) Before they can begin unwrapping each team must have a Park Patrol member visually check to see that Lazarus is completely wrapped. Then they must unwrap Lazarus (not rip off the covering). The first team to finish is the winner.

LESSON 27 SNACK:
Energy Bars

Supplies: An energy or granola type bar or another "quick energy" snack, such as trail mix, raisins, or fruit slices

Directions: Gather the children to the snack area. Have the Park Patrol pass out snacks to the children. If using some type of energy bars, you may want to divide them in half or into fourths. As the children eat the snack remind them that a snack that gives them power can remind them that Jesus is all-powerful.

LESSON 27 PRESCHOOL GAME:
Unwrap Lazarus

Supplies: Roll of toilet tissue or crepe paper streamer · Noah's Park leader

Directions: Right before playing the game, wrap several lengths of tissue or paper around a leader. The more pieces wrapped on the leader, the longer the game will take.

After Lazarus came out of the cave, his friends helped take off all the cloths he had been wrapped in before he was buried. Let's pretend (leader's name) is Lazarus. We are his friends. We need to unwrap him. Have the children take turns unwrapping "Lazarus." While they are unwrapping, they could sing the following song to the tune of "The Farmer in the Dell."

Unwrap friend Lazarus,
Unwrap friend Lazarus.
Jesus made him come alive,
Unwrap friend Lazarus.

LESSON 28 SNACK:
Blind Taste Test

Supplies: Brown paper lunch bags · Four or five small, dry snacks (dry cereal, cookies, fish crackers, raisins, etc.) · Optional: a variety of beverages (apple juice, soda pop, water, etc.) and cups

Preparation: Place each snack in its own bag and set the bags spread out on a table. Make sure the children do not look inside them.

Directions: Children take turns closing their eyes, reaching in a bag to pull out a treat, and eating it without looking at it first. Children will taste their treat before they know what it is. Encourage children to not give away the secret of what's in the bags. (Be aware of any children with food allergies!)

As an option, you could do a similar taste test with beverages. Use cups that are not clear and have the children taste before looking at what they are drinking.

LESSON 28 ELEMENTARY GAME:
Blindfolded Obstacle Course

Supplies: Obstacles (tables, chairs, waste baskets, empty boxes, or appropriate classroom items) · Blindfolds

Preparation: Set up a short, simple obstacle course. You might include tables to crawl under, chairs to climb over, wastebaskets to circle around, or rows of chairs to form a zigzag walk.

Directions: Choose one child to be blindfolded and begin as "the blind man." The blind man must walk through the obstacle course asking for help from the other kids, who line the sides. The kids should not give directions or advice unless the blind man asks for help. When the child has completed the obstacle course, let another child have a turn. If the children who have their turn near the end begin to memorize the course from having watched it a few times, alter the course after blindfolding them.

LESSON 28 SNACK:
Blind Taste Test

Supplies: Brown paper lunch bags · Four or five small, dry snacks (dry cereal, cookies, fish crackers, raisins, etc.) · Optional: a variety of beverages (apple juice, soda pop, water, etc.) and cups

Preparation: Place each snack in its own bag and set the bags spread out on a table. Make sure the children do not look inside them.

Directions: Children take turns closing their eyes, reaching in a bag to pull out a treat, and eating it without looking at it first. Children will taste their treat before they know what it is. Encourage children to not give away the secret of what's in the bags. (Be aware of any children with food allergies!)

As an option, you could do a similar taste test with beverages. Use cups that are not clear and have the children taste before looking at what they are drinking.

LESSON 28 PRESCHOOL GAME:
Blind Man's Echo Tag

Supplies: Blindfold · Ponder the Frog puppet

Directions: Have the children sit in a circle. Choose one child to be the "blind man" and blindfold him or her. The blind man stands in the middle of the circle. Choose another child to be inside the circle, not blindfolded. That child wears the Ponder the Frog puppet. The object of the game is for the blind man to catch the child holding Ponder.

Whenever the blind man calls, **"Who's coming?"** the child wearing Ponder must answer, **"Jesus. And He can help you."** The blindfolded child moves around in the circle, following the voice of the other child, who quietly tries to move away. When the blind man touches the child wearing Ponder, choose two other children to be in the circle.

LESSON 29 SNACK:
Floating Fruit

Supplies: Large bowls of water · Snacks that will float on water (apple slices, banana chunks, celery sticks, etc.) · Large slotted spoons · Small paper plates

Directions: Put the fruit in the bowl of water and set it where the children can reach it. Ask the children how a floating snack can remind them to trust Jesus. *(When Peter was trusting Jesus, he stayed on top of the water.)* Let the children use slotted spoons to fish out snacks and set them on their plates.

LESSON 29 ELEMENTARY GAME:
Trust Tag

Supplies: Blindfolds

Directions: Have each child get together with a partner. If it doesn't work out evenly, have a Park Patrol helper be a child's partner. Blindfold one child in each pair. The seeing partner is to direct the blind partner by holding his or her shoulders and giving verbal clues. The blind partner tries to tag another blind person. The blind partner has to trust the seeing partner to guide and keep him or her from being tagged by others. Remind the children to play gently—the partner who is not blindfolded needs to be careful not to push or pull the blind partner around. Set a time limit for the game (about two minutes), and let the pairs see how many other pairs they can tag. Then have the children switch roles and play again.

LESSON 29 SNACK:
Floating Fruit

Supplies: Large bowls of water · Snacks that will float on water (apple slices, banana chunks, celery sticks, etc.) · Large slotted spoons · Small paper plates

Directions: Put the fruit in the bowl of water and set it where the children can reach it. Ask the children how a floating snack can remind them to trust Jesus. *(When Peter was trusting Jesus, he stayed on top of the water.)* Let the children use slotted spoons to fish out snacks and set them on their plates.

LESSON 29 PRESCHOOL GAME:
Leap to the Boat

Supplies: Masking tape

Preparation: Make a simple boat shape on the floor using the masking tape. Make a separate tape line about 10 feet from the boat for the start line.

Directions: Have the children stand behind the start line.

Jesus walked on the water. Then Jesus invited Peter to walk on the water too. Peter did as Jesus asked. Pretend that the space between the line and the boat is water. Let's see if you can follow directions like Peter did. Try to get to the boat using the action I tell you.

Give each child an action to use to get to the boat. Children should go one at a time. Some possible actions are walking, leaping, hopping, jumping, skipping, running.

Those children who have reached the boat can encourage those trying to get to the boat

LESSON 30 SNACK:
Progressive Snack

Supplies: Plates · Crackers · Cheese spread or peanut butter · Plastic knives · Cups · Drink

Directions: Have the kids travel from area to area to put together their snacks. This will remind the children that Jesus traveled from town to town. Set the plates out in the first area, the crackers at the next area, the cheese spread or peanut butter with plastic knives next, the cups at yet another area, and the drink to pour into the cups last. (Be sure that any children with nut allergies do not touch the peanut butter.)

LESSON 30 ELEMENTARY GAME:
Shoe Search

Supplies: None

Directions: Have the children sit in a circle and take off one shoe. Play the Unit Song, "Greatest Love," while the children pass the shoes around the circle. When the music stops, have the children place the shoe they are holding on the floor in front of them. Then have the children remove their other shoe and again pass it around the circle in the other direction as the music plays again. When the music stops, most children will have two different shoes in front of them.

Now the kids take the shoes in front of them and put them in different places around the room. Remind the children not to hide the shoes, but to place them where they can be found. Then the kids return to the circle. Remind the children that Jesus traveled by foot to many different places to teach people about God. Tell the children that in order to get their shoes back, they will need to travel to different places in the room. When you give the signal, the children walk to get their shoes, put them on, and return to the circle. (**This game is not a race!**)

LESSON 30 SNACK:

Progressive Snack

Supplies: Plates · Crackers · Cheese spread or peanut butter · Plastic knives · Cups · Drink

Directions: Have the kids travel from area to area to put together their snacks. This will remind the children that Jesus traveled from town to town. Set the plates out in the first area, the crackers at next area, the cheese spread or peanut butter with plastic knives next, the cups at yet another area, and the drink to pour into the cups last. (Be sure that any children with nut allergies do not touch the peanut butter.)

LESSON 30 PRESCHOOL GAME:

Traveling Relay Game

Supplies: Two backpacks or duffel bags · Paper · Marker · Masking tape

Preparation: Print a large "S" on a piece of paper, and a large "H" on another. Tape them in two different parts of your playing area. With masking tape, mark two start lines on the floor at the opposite end of the room from the signs.

Directions: Divide children into two teams. Have each team stand behind a start line. **Let's pretend that we are Jesus' helpers. We are traveling with Him. First we'll go to the synagogue.** Point to the "S" sign, and have the children say "synagogue." **Then we'll travel to Peter's house.** Point to the "H" sign, and have the children say "house." **Finally, we'll travel back to this line.** The players on each team will take turns carrying their backpack to each place and then coming back to the start line. The first team to have all their players travel around, wins.

Be sure children understand the directions. Give the first child in each line a backpack. Park Patrol helpers can help direct the children as they travel. When the first child completes the route, he or she gives the backpack to the next child, who walks the same route. Continue until all the children have had a turn. *(Even if one team finishes first, let the other team finish playing so all get to play.)*

LESSON 31 SNACK:
Fruity Snacks

Supplies: Fruit that contains seeds (apples, kiwi, strawberries, watermelon, pomegranate, etc.) · Sharp knife · Small paper plates

Directions: Before cutting up the fruit, talk with the children about what's inside *(seeds)*. Explain that some seeds can be eaten and others cannot. Cut the fruit into bite-size pieces, and put some on each plate. Encourage the children to try new fruits. **Be sure to check for food allergies (such as strawberries) among the children.**

LESSON 31 ELEMENTARY GAME:
Farmer Says

Supplies: None

Directions: This game is similar to "Simon Says." Have the children stand and spread out in the room, facing you. As you give various fun commands, the children must listen carefully for the words, "Jesus says." When you say, "Farmer says," before a command, the kids should follow the command. If you say any other name (like that of a child in your class), the children should just stand still.

The children don't have to sit out if they make a mistake. Instead, see how long the group can play without anyone making a mistake. Suggestions for commands: **clap your hands three times, say the memory verse, hop on your left foot, shake your neighbor's hand, nod your head and jump up twice, pat your head and rub your tummy, say the name of the church, do four jumping jacks, and so on.**

LESSON 31 SNACK:
Fruity Snacks

Supplies: Fruit that contains seeds (apples, kiwi, strawberries, watermelon, pomegranate, etc.) · Sharp knife · Small paper plates

Directions: Before cutting up the fruit, talk with the children about what's inside *(seeds)*. Explain that some seeds can be eaten and others cannot. Cut the fruit into bite-size pieces, and put some on each plate. Encourage the children to try new fruits. **Be sure to check for food allergies (such as strawberries) among the children.**

LESSON 31 PRESCHOOL GAME:
Scattering Seeds

Supplies: Beanbags or soft balls, one for each child

Directions: Have the children stand in a large, spread-out circle. Give each child a beanbag or ball. **Let's pretend that our balls are the seeds from the Bible story. We are the farmers. Throw your seeds into the circle.** Let the children throw the balls. **Birds ate the seeds that fell on the path. Can you be birds, and fly over and pick up one seed?** Children don't need to pick up the same ball that they threw. Have them return to their spot in the circle.

Now let's throw your seeds again. Let the children throw. **They fell on rocks this time! Pretend to climb over the rocks as you go pick up a seed.** Have the children retrieve balls again.

Throw the seeds again! Let the children throw. **Look, they fell on thorns. Walk carefully to get a ball without pricking yourself.** The children may say, "Ouch!" as they pick up a ball.

Throw your seeds once more. Let the children throw. **Now stoop down low and stretch up high to show how your seeds fell on good soil and grew and grew and grew.** Have the children do this. If time permits, repeat the game.

LESSON 32 SNACK:

Heart Treats

Supplies: Cheese slices · Heart-shaped cookie cutter · Red gelatin · Optional: candy hearts

Preparation: Make a pan of red gelatin and cut into heart shapes

Directions: Before starting the snack, pray to thank Jesus for His love. As the children eat, talk about ways to remember during the week that Jesus loves them.

LESSON 32 ELEMENTARY GAME:

Show Love to Zacchaeus

Supplies: Chair

Directions: This game is similar to "Red Light, Green Light." Place a chair at one end of the room. Choose one child to be Zacchaeus up in the tree. This child stands on the chair with his back to the kids. (Have an adult nearby for safety.) The rest of the group lines up at the opposite end of the room. The goal is to be the first one to "show love to Zacchaeus" and help him down from the tree.

Zacchaeus says "green light" and the kids may move forward (only by walking). When Zacchaeus says "red light," the children must stop immediately. Zacchaeus turns around and tries to catch any child still in motion. If Zacchaeus sees someone still moving, that child must go back to the starting line. The first child to touch Zacchaeus helps him down and becomes the new Zacchaeus. Play again as time allows.

LESSON 32 SNACK:
Heart Treats

Supplies: Cheese slices · Heart-shaped cookie cutter · Red gelatin · Optional: candy hearts

Preparation: Make a pan of red gelatin and cut into heart shapes

Directions: Before starting the snack, pray to thank Jesus for His love. As the children eat, talk about ways to remember during the week that Jesus loves them.

LESSON 32 PRESCHOOL GAME:
Friend-to-Friend Game

Supplies: None

Directions: Choose one child to be the leader while the rest of the children divide into pairs. If a child doesn't have a partner, you or a Park Patrol helper could join the group.

Jesus showed His love to Zacchaeus. Zacchaeus learned how to be a friend to others. Let's play a game with friends. Call out parts of the body, such as elbows, ankles, fingers, or toes. The pairs touch those parts together. After naming a few body parts, have the leader call, **"Switch to another friend."** The children should switch partners.

LESSON 33 SNACK:
Kingly Treats

Supplies: "Kingly" treats, such as any cereal with the word "gold" in the name or homemade cookies in a crown shape, etc.

Directions: As the children eat, talk about how their "kingly" snack can remind them that Jesus is King.

LESSON 33 ELEMENTARY GAME:
The King's Rules

Supplies: Toy or paper crown

Directions: Choose one child to be the "king." Divide the rest of the children into two groups. The king gets to make one law, and the two teams see which can obey it the fastest. The law can be a way for the kids to arrange themselves or a shape or task to do together. For example, the king might tell the groups to arrange themselves in order of birthdays, alphabetically by first name, or smallest to tallest. Or the king might tell them to form a figure eight (as a group) or sit in a circle with all their toes touching.

The first group to obey the king's law wins. The king gives his or her crown to somebody from the winning team, and the old king joins that team. Play several times so different children get to be king. Be on hand to give the kings suggestions.

LESSON 33 SNACK:
Kingly Treats

Supplies: "Kingly" treats, such as any cereal with the word "gold" in the name or homemade cookies in a crown shape, etc.

Directions: As the children eat, talk about how their "kingly" snack can remind them that Jesus is King.

LESSON 33 PRESCHOOL GAME:
Group Musical Chairs

Supplies: Chairs · Noah's Park CD and CD player

Directions: Set up chairs in two rows, back to back. Have one chair for each child. Have the children stand in a circle around the chairs and begin walking when you play the CD. Randomly pause the CD. The children all sit in the closest chair. (Everyone should have a chair on the first round.) Ask the children to stand as you remove a chair from each row. Have the children walk to the music again. This time, when the music stops, everyone races for a chair. The two children who don't have chairs need to sit on the closest lap. Remove two more chairs, and repeat, with four children finding laps. Play until only two chairs are left.

LESSON 34 SNACK:
Jesus Lives

Supplies: Pretzels or string licorice · Paper plates

Directions: Today's snack involves spelling out the words: "JESUS LIVES." Print the words on the board so the children will spell it correctly. Give each child a paper plate. Place pretzels or string licorice where all can reach them. The children may break or bend the treats into the proper shapes to form the letters. For younger children, have them make only the letters in "JESUS." Have the Park Patrol on hand to offer help as needed. After spelling, the children may eat their letters.

LESSON 34 ELEMENTARY GAME:
Spread the News Tag

Supplies: None

Directions: Choose one child to be either "Mary" or "John" and have that child stand in the middle of the room or playing area. Divide the rest of the children into two groups, and have them stand on opposite sides of the room. At your signal, the children run to the other side of the room, trying not to be tagged by "Mary" or "John." As "John" or "Mary" tags them, he or she must tell them, "Jesus lives!"

The child or children tagged hold hands with "John" or "Mary" to make a chain (they cannot unlink their arms). Only the children on the end can reach out and tag people, but they must tell any child tagged, "Jesus lives!" When all the loose children have reached the opposite wall, give the signal again, and let the children try to get to the other side. Continue playing until all the children have been tagged and told that Jesus lives. If you have enough time, chose a new "Mary" or "John" and let the kids play again.

LESSON 34 SNACK:
Jesus Lives

Supplies: Pretzels or string licorice · Paper plates

Directions: Today's snack involves spelling out the words: "JESUS LIVES." Print the words on the board so the children will spell it correctly. Give each child a paper plate. Place pretzels or string licorice where all can reach them. The children may break or bend the treats into the proper shapes to form the letters. For younger children, have them make only the letters in "JESUS." Have the Park Patrol on hand to offer help as needed. After spelling, the children may eat their letters.

LESSON 34 PRESCHOOL GAME:
Find the Cloth

Supplies: White cloth

Preparation: Hide a white cloth in your area.

Directions: Gather the children in a circle around you. **When the women went to the cave, they found that Jesus was alive again. The angel told them to look in the cave. When they looked in the cave, they might have looked for a white cloth—the clothes that Jesus had been buried in. There is a white cloth hidden in our room. Can you find it?**

Encourage the children to look for the cloth. The child who finds the cloth should bring it back to the circle area. Continue playing the game by having the child who found the cloth hide it again.

LESSON 35 SNACK:
Bible Grahams

Supplies: Graham crackers · Tube frosting

Directions: Give each child two graham crackers hooked together. This represents the Bible. Let the kids use the tube of frosting to write "BIBLE" on their graham cracker Bible. As the children wait for their turn to use the frosting, let them share their favorite Bible stories.

LESSON 35 ELEMENTARY GAME:
Teacher Scramble

Supplies: None

Directions: Divide the children into four groups. Give each group a name of someone who teaches them about Jesus: parents, pastor, Sunday school teacher, or children's church teacher. Make sure the children remember their group name. Practice by pointing from group to group and have them shout their group name. Then have each child bring a chair to make a large circle. Remove one chair and have that child stand in the middle of the circle. Have the rest of the children mix up their places so all the kids in one group are not seated together.

To play, the child in the middle calls out one of the group names: parents, pastor, Sunday school teacher, or children's church teacher. Whichever group is called, the children in that group jump up and rush to change seats. At the same time, the child in the middle also tries to get one of the seats. One child will be left standing. That child becomes the person who calls another group. If the child in the middle calls, "All teachers!" all of the children jump up and switch seats. Play several times to allow several children a chance to be in the middle.

LESSON 35 SNACK:
Bible Grahams

Supplies: Graham crackers · Tube frosting

Directions: Give each child two graham crackers hooked together. This represents the Bible. Let the kids use the tube of frosting to write "BIBLE" on their graham cracker Bible. As the children wait for their turn to use the frosting, let them share their favorite Bible stories.

LESSON 35 PRESCHOOL GAME:
Teaching Relay

Supplies: Cardboard tube

Directions: Divide the children into two groups. Put the groups at opposite ends of the room. **Philip taught the man in the chariot what the words on the Bible scroll meant. Let's pretend to pass a scroll to each other. When you hand someone the scroll, be a teacher and say, "Jesus loves you."**

Give the first child in one line the cardboard tube. That child hops to the first person in the other line, says, **"Jesus loves you,"** and hands over the tube. The new child to hold the tube hops back to the first group and hands off the tube while saying, **"Jesus loves you."** Continue playing with the children taking turns. The relay is over when all the children have moved the cardboard tube.

The relay can be repeated using other actions such as galloping or walking quickly.

LESSON 36 SNACK:
Spelling Snack

Supplies: Alphabet cereal · Pretzel sticks · Plates · Napkins

Directions: Give each child a napkin, and spread out alphabet cereal and pretzel sticks on plates where all can see them. Encourage the children to each spell the word "help" before eating their snack. Also encourage the children to work together to find the right cereal letters or form the right pretzel letters.

LESSON 36 ELEMENTARY GAME:
Bucket Brigade

Supplies: Four large containers · Water · Cup for each child · Towels

Directions: The object of the game is for two teams to form a bucket brigade and help each other get the water from one end of the line to the other.

Divide the children into two teams and have them line up. Place a container of water at one end of each team. Place an empty container at the other end of each team. At your signal, the player on each team closest to the water dips some out and pours it into the next person's cup. The water should be passed from cup to cup until the last person pours it into the container at the end. When both teams are done, measure and see which team has the most water in the container at the end. Have towels on hand to clean up spills.

LESSON 36 SNACK:
Spelling Snack

Supplies: Alphabet cereal · Pretzel sticks · Plates · Napkins

Directions: Give each child a napkin, and spread out alphabet cereal and pretzel sticks on plates where all can see them. Encourage the children to each spell the word "help" before eating their snack. Also encourage the children to work together to find the right cereal letters or form the right pretzel letters.

LESSON 36 PRESCHOOL GAME:
Clothes Relay

Supplies: Two adult-size shirts or coats

Directions: Divide the children into two groups. Have the groups stand at one end of the game area. Place the shirts or coats at the opposite end of the area. **Dorcas helped people by sewing clothes for them. When it is your turn, run to the shirt, put it on, and then take it off again. Leave the shirt there and run back to your team.** Let the children run the relay, one at a time, until all the children have had a turn.

LESSON 37 SNACK:
Gingerbread Men

Supplies: Gingerbread man cookies or other people-shaped cookies or crackers

Directions: As the children eat their people-shaped treat, encourage them to talk about who is in their family. A Noah's Park puppet could visit with the children to tell them about animal families.

LESSON 37 ELEMENTARY GAME:
Grab the Bag

Supplies: Paper bag · Tape · Wadded-up newspaper

Directions: Fill a paper bag with wadded-up newspaper, and tape it shut. Write on both sides: "Families can help us know Jesus."

This game is similar to "Steal the Bacon." Divide the kids into two equal teams. You or a Park Patrol member can join a team to make an equal number if necessary. Have the teams line up on opposite sides of the room. Have the players on each team number off and remember their number, for example 1-10. (Both teams will have players with the same numbers.)

Set the paper bag in the middle of the room. Call out a number. The child from each team with that number races to grab the bag first and return it to their team. Whichever team gets the bag calls out together, "Families can help us know Jesus!" Return the bag to the center, call out a different number, and play again. Continue until all the kids have had a chance to try to grab the bag.

LESSON 37 SNACK:
Gingerbread Men

Supplies: Gingerbread man cookies or other people-shaped cookies or crackers

Directions: As the children eat their people-shaped treat, encourage them to talk about who is in their family. A Noah's Park puppet could visit with the children to tell them about animal families.

LESSON 37 PRESCHOOL GAME:
Timothy, May I?

Supplies: None

Directions: Choose one child to be Timothy. Timothy stands at one end of the room while the rest of the children wait at the other end. **In our Bible story, Timothy helped Paul tell people about Jesus. The Timothy in our game is going to help us get to the other side of our room.**

The children take turns asking, **"Timothy, may I take __ steps?"** They fill in the blank with any number or type of step they wish, such as "eight baby steps" or "three bunny hops." Timothy answers either, **"Yes, you may,"** or gives an alternative, such as, **"No, but you may take four giant steps."** The children then take that number and type of steps. After enough questions, one child will reach Timothy. He or she becomes the new Timothy, and the game begins again.

LESSON 38 SNACK:
Teamwork Trail Mix

Supplies: Four or five snack items (popcorn, peanuts, raisins, chocolate chips, candies, mini pretzels, etc.) · Serving spoon or scoop and container for each ingredient · Serving bowl or large plastic food bag for every four to five children · Small plates or napkins

Directions: Set out the ingredients in separate containers, with a serving spoon or scoop in each. Divide the kids into groups of four or five. Give each group a serving bowl or plastic food bag. Each child from each group gets a scoop of one ingredient and brings it back to their bowl or bag. Each group should end up with one scoop of every ingredient. Have the kids mix then equally divide the snack among all group members.

Point out how each ingredient tastes good alone but they all taste better when "working together."

LESSON 38 ELEMENTARY GAME:
Turn the Gears

Supplies: None

Directions: Divide the children into at least three groups of four or more kids in a group. Have the Park Patrol helpers join in the game. Have the kids in each circle link arms at the elbows.

Assign one circle to be the main gear. Bring a second circle next to the first circle so they are just touching. Each child will be a tooth in the gear. One child fits perfectly in the gap between two children from the other gear. Then bring the third (or more) circles close enough to touch the second gear.

Tell the first gear to begin to turn. Everyone in that circle begins to move to the right. As the first gear begins to turn, it will start the second gear turning, which will start the third gear turning. As long as the gears work together, the game moves smoothly. As the children grow accustomed to how the pattern works, you may tell the gears to stop, change direction, speed up, or slow down.

LESSON 38 SNACK:
Teamwork Trail Mix

Supplies: Four or five snack items (popcorn, peanuts, raisins, chocolate chips, candies, mini pretzels, etc.) · Serving spoon or scoop and container for each ingredient · Serving bowl or large plastic food bag for every four to five children · Small plates or napkins

Directions: Set out the ingredients in separate containers, with a serving spoon or scoop in each. Divide the kids into groups of four or five. Give each group a serving bowl or plastic food bag. Each child from each group gets a scoop of one ingredient and brings it back to their bowl or bag. Each group should end up with one scoop of every ingredient. Have the kids mix then equally divide the snack among all group members.

Point out how each ingredient tastes good alone but they all taste better when "working together."

LESSON 38 PRESCHOOL GAME:
Working Together Relay

Supplies: Blocks

Directions: Divide the blocks into two equal piles and place them at one end of the room. Divide the children into two groups and have them stand at the opposite end of the room.

Jesus' friends work together. Can you work together to build a tower of blocks? One at a time, have the children run to get a block from their team's pile, bring it back and use it to build a tower. Encourage the children to work together instead of having one team build faster than the other.

If you have a small class, do the activity with one group.

LESSON 39 SNACK:
"J" Is for Jesus

Supplies: Crackers · Squeeze cheese or squeeze cream cheese · Napkins

Directions: Ask the children what letter the name "Jesus" begins with. When they answer "J," show them how to draw a letter J on a cracker using the squeeze cheese. Let each child prepare his or her own crackers.

As the children eat, let them each tell one thing they know about Jesus.

LESSON 39 ELEMENTARY GAME:
Clothespin Race

Supplies: Clothespins (three or four per child)

Directions: Give each child three or four clothespins (the same number for every child). Explain that the children must race to pin their clothespins on other children while telling something they know about Jesus. At the same time, the children try to avoid getting pinned by others.

Explain that the children need to stop moving while someone is pinning a clothespin on them and telling them about Jesus. Only one person at a time may attach a clothespin. Each child's clothespins must go to four (or five) different children. (Things the children might "tell" about Jesus include: Jesus is King, Jesus loves you, Jesus died for your sins, Jesus is God's Son, Jesus was born in Bethlehem, Jesus hears your prayers, and so on.)

Set a time limit, such as two minutes, and give the signal to begin. As the children play, remind them of the rules as necessary. When time is up, have the children pull off all the clothespins and see how many people told them about Jesus.

LESSON 39 SNACK:
"J" Is for Jesus

Supplies: Crackers · Squeeze cheese or squeeze cream cheese · Napkins

Directions: Ask the children what letter the name "Jesus" begins with. When they answer "J," show them how to draw a letter J on a cracker using the squeeze cheese. Let each child prepare his or her own crackers.

As the children eat, let them each tell one thing they know about Jesus.

LESSON 39 PRESCHOOL GAME:
Friend Tag

Supplies: Noah's Park puppet

Directions: Choose one child to be "IT" and wear a Noah's Park puppet. Explain to the class that the puppet wants to be their friend and will try and tag every child. When tagged, the child needs to give the puppet a hug.

Let "IT" try to tag the children within a designated area. When a child is tagged, he or she should hug the Noah's Park puppet. Play until everyone has hugged the puppet. Then pick a new child to be "IT" and play again. If you have a large group, let each child who hugs the puppet become "IT" until he or she tags someone else.

LESSON 40 SNACK:
Manna and Milk

Supplies: Oyster crackers (small, round, salty crackers) · Napkins
· Milk (white or chocolate) · Cups

Directions: Explain that we don't really know what manna tasted like, but that the Book of Exodus describes it as being like bread. Have kids put their heads on their arms on the table, as if they're napping, then sprinkle a handful of oyster crackers on each child's napkin. They can pretend they're the Israelites who wake up to manna on the ground, covered by dew each morning. Offer milk (or water) to go with their "manna."

LESSON 40 ELEMENTARY GAME:
Manna, Quail

Supplies: Masking tape or crepe paper

Directions: Make a line down the center of your playing area with a strip of masking tape or crepe paper. Assign one side of the line to be "manna" and the other side to be "quail." The children may stand on either side of the line to begin.

When you call out "manna," the children must jump to the manna side of the line. When you call out "quail," the children must jump to the other side. Whoever jumps to the wrong side steps out of the game for this round. Call out "manna" and "quail" quickly, and mix them up, to keep the kids hopping and listening carefully. Repeat the game as time allows.

LESSON 40 SNACK:
Manna and Milk

Supplies: Oyster crackers (small, round, salty crackers) · Napkins · Milk (white or chocolate) · Cups

Directions: Explain that we don't really know what manna tasted like, but that the Book of Exodus describes it as being like bread. Have kids put their heads on their arms on the table, as if they're napping, then sprinkle a handful of oyster crackers on each child's napkin. They can pretend they're the Israelites who wake up to manna on the ground, covered by dew each morning. Offer milk (or water) to go with their "manna."

LESSON 40 PRESCHOOL GAME:
Manna Gather Relay

Supplies: Crumpled newspaper balls · Large basket · Noah's Park puppet

Directions: Have the children stand in a line, side by side. Put the crumpled newspaper balls at one end of the line and the basket at the other end. Ask one child to stand next to the basket with the Noah's Park puppet on a hand.

The children take one crumpled newspaper at a time and pass it down the line to the basket. Each child should touch each ball. When it gets to the basket, the child with the puppet helps to count each newspaper ball. The relay ends when all the newspaper balls are in the basket and counted.

LESSON 41 SNACK:
Walking Stick Dip

Supplies: Healthy foods to dip, such as carrot sticks, celery sticks, pretzel sticks · One or two soft dips, such as peanut butter dip (two parts peanut butter mixed well with one part honey) or cheese dip (add a handful of shredded Cheddar cheese to a container of Ranch-style dip) · Napkins · Cups of water

Directions: Place small containers of the dips on tables where all the children can reach them. Explain what flavors the dips are. If you choose a peanut butter dip, be sure to check ahead of time for children who may have a nut allergy and plan to offer them another choice.

Let the children choose "walking sticks" (carrots, celery, pretzels) to dip in "pools of water" (the dips). Talk with the children about how Moses used his walking stick to hit the rock, as God instructed him, and water poured out of the rock.

LESSON 41 ELEMENTARY GAME:
Water Relay

Supplies: Two plastic cups of the same size · Four buckets · Water

Directions: Divide class into two teams, and have each team form a line. Place a nearly full bucket of water in front of each team. At the opposite end of your playing area, place two empty buckets, one across from each team.

At your signal, the first player on each team grabs a cup, scoops up water from the bucket, and quickly walks to the empty bucket across from their team. These players then dump in their water, walk quickly back, and hand the cup to the next person in their line, who then takes a turn. Encourage walking rather than running to minimize slipping on spilled water. Continue the relay for a set amount of time, such as two minutes. The team with the most water in their far bucket wins.

LESSON 41 SNACK:
Walking Stick Dip

Supplies: Healthy foods to dip, such as carrot sticks, celery sticks, pretzel sticks · One or two soft dips, such as peanut butter dip (two parts peanut butter mixed well with one part honey) or cheese dip (add a handful of shredded Cheddar cheese to a container of Ranch-style dip) · Napkins · Cups of water

Directions: Place small containers of the dips on tables where all the children can reach them. Explain what flavors the dips are. If you choose a peanut butter dip, be sure to check ahead of time for children who may have a nut allergy and plan to offer them another choice.

Let the children choose "walking sticks" (carrots, celery, pretzels) to dip in "pools of water" (the dips). Talk with the children about how Moses used his walking stick to hit the rock, as God instructed him, and water poured out of the rock.

LESSON 41 PRESCHOOL GAME:
Puddle Jumping

Supplies: Carpet squares (Option: construction paper taped to the floor)

Directions: Lay the carpet squares in a line. Leave enough space between the squares for children to stand.

After water came out of the rock, there may have been puddles on the ground. Let's play a puddle game. Have the children take turns hopping, jumping, and walking across the puddles. Encourage the children to come up with their own ways of getting across the puddles.

LESSON 42 SNACK:
Camel's Lips

Supplies: Smooth peanut butter · Red apple slices · Plastic knife · Napkins

Directions: Abraham would probably have traveled with camels. Make a silly snack of Camel's Lips by spreading some peanut butter on one slice of apple, then topping it with a second apple slice. The apples (skin side out) are the lips, the peanut butter the tongue.

If you have children with nut allergies, you may substitute marshmallow crème.

LESSON 42 ELEMENTARY GAME:
Abraham Says

Supplies: None

Directions: This game is a version of "Simon Says." Stand facing the group. Give simple commands. If you say, **"Abraham says,"** before any command, the children are to do what you say. If you give a command without saying "Abraham says," the children should not do what you say.

Commands you give the children should be fun, such as jumping in place, patting their heads, turning around, or shaking another's hand. You may try to be tricky to encourage good listening skills. Children who make a mistake must be seated for the remainder of that round. Play several rounds.

After playing, remind children that Abraham had to listen to God and do what God said to follow God's plan. We also have to listen and obey if we want to know and follow God's plan.

LESSON 42 SNACK:
Camel's Lips

Supplies: Smooth peanut butter · Red apple slices · Plastic knife · Napkins

Directions: Abraham would probably have traveled with camels. Make a silly snack of Camel's Lips by spreading some peanut butter on one slice of apple, then topping it with a second apple slice. The apples (skin side out) are the lips, the peanut butter the tongue.

If you have children with nut allergies, you may substitute marshmallow crème.

LESSON 42 PRESCHOOL GAME:
Duffel Bag Relay

Supplies: Two duffel bags or soft-sided suitcases · Two identical sets of non-breakable traveling items for each bag (small clothing, hairbrush, book, etc.)

Directions: Divide the children into two groups. If you have a very small group, use just one duffel bag. Have the groups stand in single-file lines at one end of the room. Place the duffel bags at the other end of the room with the objects next to them.

God told Abraham to move to a new land. Let's help him pack. The first child in each line should run to a bag, place all of the objects inside, and run to the back of their line. Then pause and say, **Abraham and his family are at their new land. Let's help them unpack.** Now the second child in each line runs to the bag, unpacks the whole thing, and runs back to their line.

Continue having the children pack and unpack the bags until each child has had a turn.

LESSON 43 SNACK:
Yummy Promises Chain

Supplies: Cereal with holes in the center · Licorice laces (or string)

Directions: Place containers of cereal within reach of the children. Give each child a length of licorice (or string) on which to string some cereal. The strings of treats can be knotted into necklaces if desired. Children can eat their creations and take home the leftovers, if any.

LESSON 43 ELEMENTARY GAME:
Link Tag

Supplies: None

Directions: Have two children link arms. Everyone else scatters around the room. The linked pair moves around the room, trying to tag individual kids, who then join the chain. The kids in the chain may not break their links, and only the kids on the two ends will have a hand free to reach out and tag. The unlinked kids may run away to avoid being tagged, but as the chain grows longer, this will become harder to do. Play until the chain breaks or until every child is linked. In either case, start over with a new pair to begin another round, as time permits.

LESSON 43 SNACK:
Yummy Promises Chain

Supplies: Cereal with holes in the center · Licorice laces (or string)

Directions: Place containers of cereal within reach of the children. Give each child a length of licorice (or string) on which to string some cereal. The strings of treats can be knotted into necklaces if desired. Children can eat their creations and take home the leftovers, if any.

LESSON 43 PRESCHOOL GAME:
Stars in the Sky

Supplies: None

Directions: Choose a child to be Abraham. Tell the rest of the children that they are stars. Whisper a number to Abraham. It may be any number between one and twenty. Abraham sits in the middle of a circle formed by the other children, who are the stars. You will need to have a "safe" zone off to the side of your circle. The stars march in a circle around Abraham, counting together as they march. When they say the number you had whispered, Abraham, jumps up and tries to tag as many stars as possible before they run to the safe zone. The stars that are tagged stay by Abraham.

Continue the game choosing another Abraham. Use a different number for each Abraham.

LESSON 44 SNACK:
Elijah's Bagel Bits

Supplies: Plain bagels · Flavored cream cheese · Plastic knives · Cups of water

Preparation: Cut the bagels in half and then cut each half into fourths.

Directions: Remind the children that God provided bread and water for Elijah and the widow. Let the children sample the plain bagel and water. Then let those who wish spread cream cheese on their bagel bits.

LESSON 44 ELEMENTARY GAME:
Share-a-thon

Supplies: Containers (baskets, small boxes, shallow bowls), one per child · 10 identical small objects per child, such as craft sticks, pencils, small paper balls, etc.

Directions: Each player begins with a container and 10 small objects. Everyone spreads out around the playing area and places their container of objects near their feet. The goal is to share or give away all the objects in their basket by running around and placing them in other kids' containers. No more than two objects may be placed in another's container at a time. While players put items in others' containers, their own containers will receive more items, which they retrieve and share again. Play until someone's container is empty or the children are tired.

LESSON 44 SNACK:
Elijah's Bagel Bits

Supplies: Plain bagels · Flavored cream cheese · Plastic knives · Cups of water

Preparation: Cut the bagels in half and then cut each half into fourths.

Directions: Remind the children that God provided bread and water for Elijah and the widow. Let the children sample the plain bagel and water. Then let those who wish spread cream cheese on their bagel bits.

LESSON 44 PRESCHOOL GAME:
Bread from a Sheet

Supplies: Twin or full flat sheet (or a small parachute)

Directions: Spread the sheet on the floor. Space the children equally around the edges. Have the children bend down, grip the edge of the sheet with both hands and stand up straight again.

Elijah walked from town to town, telling people about God. The children walk in a circle holding the sheet. Then stand still.

But there was a problem. No rain had come for a long time. Everyone was hungry. Have the children shake the sheet up and down to create waves.

God sent Elijah to a woman. She shared her bread with him. Lay the sheet on the floor. Then have the children lift it up as high as possible. The next step is for all the children to quickly kneel down, bringing the edges to the floor. The air trapped inside creates a dome or loaf of bread.

There was bread again the next day. Make another loaf.

There was bread again the next day. Make another loaf.

And there was bread each day until it rained. Make another loaf of bread.

LESSON 45 SNACK:
Isaac's Wells

Supplies: Small paper or plastic cups · Blue-colored, flavored gelatin · Plastic spoons

Preparation: The day before class, prepare blue gelatin and pour into cups. Refrigerate.

Directions: Serve each child a "well" of gelatin with a "shovel" (plastic spoon) so kids can dig a well as Isaac's servants did.

LESSON 45 ELEMENTARY GAME:
Musical Chair Problems

Supplies: Chairs · Noah's Park CD and CD player

Directions: Set chairs in a circle, facing out, with one chair fewer than there are players. Play music while the children walk slowly around the circle. Stop the music at random, and have the kids race to find a seat. The child left without a chair gets to solve a "Get-Along Problem" (see suggestions below). The child should think of a positive way of getting along in the situation that you describe. If the class likes the solution, the child stays in the game. Play until most children have had a chance to solve a problem. Feel free to add your own realistic (yet simple) problems that the kids in your class would relate to.

Get-Along Problems

· On the school bus, another kid wants to sit where you're sitting. What can you do to get along?

· Your sister or brother wants to watch a different TV show than you do. What will help you get along?

· At a birthday party, you want your present to be opened first. Another guest puts his present on top of yours. What can you do to get along?

LESSON 45 SNACK:
Isaac's Wells

Supplies: Small paper or plastic cups · Blue-colored, flavored gelatin · Plastic spoons

Preparation: The day before class, prepare blue gelatin and pour into cups. Refrigerate.

Directions: Serve each child a "well" of gelatin with a "shovel" (plastic spoon) so kids can dig a well as Isaac's servants did.

LESSON 45 PRESCHOOL GAME:
Well Relay

Supplies: Three hoops or masking tape

Preparation: Put the three hoops in three different sections of the room. If you are using the tape, make three circles on the floor in different parts of the room.

Directions: Point out the hoops or circles to the class, and explain that they are wells. Have the class gather at one circle or hoop. **Isaac's neighbors made him move. When it is your turn, hop from this well to the next well.** Have all the children pretend to be Isaac and hop to the second well. **Isaac built a new well.** Have the children hop up and down 10 times. **But Isaac had to move again.** One at a time, have the children walk backward to the third well. **Again, Isaac built a new well.** Have the children do 10 jumping jacks. **This time Isaac didn't have to move. God was happy with Isaac.** Let the children jump up and down and cheer.

Challenge the children to move from well to well without having to hear the directions, one at a time. Or play the game again with different ways to "travel" between the wells.

LESSON 46 SNACK:
My Favorite Snack Mix

Supplies: Dried banana chips · Pretzel sticks · Miniature marshmallows · Small paper cups or napkins

Directions: Combine equal portions of each ingredient and mix them. Serve in small paper cups or by scooping a cupful onto each child's napkin.

Let one of your puppets oversee the snack time by talking with the children about their favorite snacks.

LESSON 46 ELEMENTARY GAME:
Joseph's Brothers Relay

Supplies: 22 beanbags or inflated balloons (11 for each team) · Two boxes for each team

Directions: Divide the class into two teams. If the number is uneven, ask a Park Patrol member to play. Have the teams line up single file, all facing in one direction. The beanbags or balloons, representing the number of brothers Joseph had, should be in a box in front of the first person. At your signal, the first person takes a beanbag and passes it between their legs to the next player. That player passes it over their head to the person behind them. The third passes it between their legs to the fourth person, who passes it over their head. Continue passing in this up-and-down fashion until the beanbag reaches the end of the line. The last player in line puts the beanbag in a box. The first team to finish wins.

LESSON 46 SNACK:
My Favorite Snack Mix

Supplies: Dried banana chips · Pretzel sticks · Miniature marshmallows · Small paper cups or napkins

Directions: Combine equal portions of each ingredient and mix them. Serve in small paper cups or by scooping a cupful onto each child's napkin.

Let one of your puppets oversee the snack time by talking with the children about their favorite snacks.

LESSON 46 PRESCHOOL GAME:
King of Egypt's Food Grab

Supplies: 10 beanbags or crumpled newspaper balls · Noah's Park puppet · Masking tape

Preparation: Make a large square on the floor using the masking tape. If space permits, make it about a 15-foot square.

Directions: Scatter the beanbags inside the square. This represents the food. Choose a child to be the King of Egypt. The king holds the puppet on a hand while standing in the middle of the square.

Say to the rest of the children, **"We are very hungry. Let's get food from Pharaoh."** The children try to get the beanbags from the square without the king tagging them with the puppet. Any child who is tagged must bring back his or her food. The game ends when all the food has been taken.

LESSON 47 SNACK:
Portable Sundaes

Supplies: Ice cream cones (mini or regular) · Vanilla pudding or yogurt · Fresh or dried fruit, each type in its own container · Large spoon · Optional: colorful sprinkles · Napkins

Preparation: If you choose the pudding option, make the pudding ahead of time.

Directions: In each person's cone, place a scoop of pudding or yogurt. Let the children show each other kindness as they pass around the containers of toppings and share with each other. The kids choose a few toppings to put on their pudding cones and then enjoy eating them.

LESSON 47 ELEMENTARY GAME:
Crazy Statues

Supplies: Noah's Park CD and CD player

Directions: Choose one child to begin as the "Spotter" and stand to the side and watch. Choose the most energetic song on the Noah's Park CD. As you play the music, the children should jump, jiggle, squirm, and in every way move their bodies around the room. No one is allowed to bump into others, however. Stop the music at random. Everyone must immediately freeze in their position—like a crazy statue. The Spotter then surveys the room, looking for anyone who moves at all (except for breathing). The first person that is spotted moving is called out to become the new Spotter. Start the music and play again. When finished playing, briefly talk with the kids about how the game reminds us of the Bible lesson—we have to sometimes really look to find those to whom we can show kindness. Challenge kids to sharpen their spotting skills this next week to find whoever needs a dose of kindness.

LESSON 47 SNACK:
Portable Sundaes

Supplies: Ice cream cones (mini or regular) · Vanilla pudding or yogurt · Fresh or dried fruit, each type in its own container · Large spoon · Optional: colorful sprinkles · Napkins

Preparation: If you choose the pudding option, make the pudding ahead of time.

Directions: In each person's cone, place a scoop of pudding or yogurt. Let the children show each other kindness as they pass around the containers of toppings and share with each other. The kids choose a few toppings to put on their pudding cones and then enjoy eating them.

LESSON 47 PRESCHOOL GAME:
Caring Pass

Supplies: Beanbag or soft ball

Directions: Have the children sit in a circle. Instruct the children to quickly pass the beanbag or ball around the circle as you lead them in singing this song, to the tune of "The Farmer in the Dell":

> **Oh, we can be kind too.**
>
> **Oh, we can be kind too.**
>
> **As David helped Mephibosheth,**
>
> **Oh, we can be kind too.**

The child holding the beanbag or ball when the singing ends gets to tell one way to be kind to someone else. Repeat as time permits.

LESSON 48 SNACK:
Ponder's Lily Pad Snackers

Supplies: Flavored cream cheese, marshmallow crème, or peanut butter · Round snack crackers or mini rice cakes · Raisins · Plastic knives

Directions: Let the children spread one of the creams on their crackers or rice cakes and then sprinkle raisins on top. Explain that the crackers or rice cakes are like lily pads and the raisins are like flies, which any frog, including Ponder, likes to eat. Check to be certain that no children in your class are allergic to peanut butter.

LESSON 48 ELEMENTARY GAME:
Oil Jug Hunt

Supplies: An assortment of empty bottles, jugs, or other non-breakable containers

Directions: Remind the class that the woman in the Bible story went on a search for jars and containers. Let the children tell how Elisha helped her. Then have the class go outside the room while you and the Park Patrol hide the containers throughout the room. (Count the containers before hiding them.) While waiting, another Park Patrol member can lead the kids in saying the Bible verse or singing a favorite song. If your group is large, divide into two teams. One team can hide the containers for the other to find, and then they can switch roles.

LESSON 48 SNACK:
Ponder's Lily Pad Snackers

Supplies: Flavored cream cheese, marshmallow crème, or peanut butter · Round snack crackers or mini rice cakes · Raisins · Plastic knives

Directions: Let the children spread one of the creams on their crackers or rice cakes and then sprinkle raisins on top. Explain that the crackers or rice cakes are like lily pads and the raisins are like flies, which any frog, including Ponder, likes to eat. Check to be certain that no children in your class are allergic to peanut butter.

LESSON 48 PRESCHOOL GAME:
Balancing Jars

Supplies: Masking tape

Preparation: Put a line of masking tape, about 10 feet long, on the floor of your game area. This will be your "balance beam."

Directions: The woman's two boys brought her empty jars to fill with oil. Pretend you are one of the boys carrying a jar to the woman. Can you walk on the balance beam to bring me a jar? Let the children walk the length of the "balance beam." Meet each child at the other end and pretend to pour oil into the jar.

Repeat the game having the children hop, skip, take giant steps, or other movements down the length of the masking tape.

LESSON 49 SNACK:
Fruit Nachos

Supplies: Pudding (any flavor) · Graham crackers · Sliced or chopped fruit (banana, apple, grapes, strawberries, etc.) · Plates · Napkins

Preparation: Make the pudding ahead of time.

Directions: Let children assemble the "nachos" by putting a graham cracker on their plate, being served a scoop of pudding, then spooning on fruit. Encourage the children to take turns and do a good job sharing.

LESSON 49 ELEMENTARY GAME:
Charades

Supplies: Paper and pen

Preparation: On slips of paper, write down jobs found in a church (secretary, janitor, choir director, teacher, food server, babysitter, gardener, usher, bus driver, etc.) or that children might do at home (make bed, pick up toys, wash dishes, sweep, fold laundry, care for pet).

Directions: Let the children each choose a slip of paper and not let anyone else see it. Help nonreaders read the job named on their paper. The kids take turns standing up and using motions to act out their job. If you would like, the children may use sounds as well, but not words. The others try to guess what the job is. You may decide to use a time limit (60 seconds) if the game is dragging.

LESSON 49 SNACK:
Fruit Nachos

Supplies: Pudding (any flavor) · Graham crackers · Sliced or chopped fruit (banana, apple, grapes, strawberries, etc.) · Plates · Napkins

Preparation: Make the pudding ahead of time.

Directions: Let children assemble the "nachos" by putting a graham cracker on their plate, being served a scoop of pudding, then spooning on fruit. Encourage the children to take turns and do a good job sharing.

LESSON 49 PRESCHOOL GAME:
Caring/Sharing Maze

Supplies: Chairs · Stuffed animal or small toy

Preparation: Set up chairs in the shape of a simple maze.

Directions: Divide the children into two groups. One group should stand at one opening of the maze. The other group should stand at the other end of the maze. **One way we can care for others is to share. When it is your turn, carry the toy through the maze to the first person in line on the other side. Then you go to the end of that line.** The child that now has the toy walks back through the maze and gives the toy to the first person on this side. Help the children walk through the maze to share the toy. Play until everyone has had a turn.

LESSON 50 SNACK:
Edible Coins

Supplies: Any round treats to represent coins (carrot slices, cucumber slices, banana slices, tortilla chips, round cookies, etc.)

Directions: To remind the children of Matthew's job as a tax collector, serve an assortment of treats that resemble coins.

LESSON 50 ELEMENTARY GAME:
Tax Collector's Relay

Supplies: Two large jars · Tokens or pennies

Directions: Make two teams of "taxpayers" who line up at one end of the room. Give each child one penny or token. Place the tax collection jars at the opposite end of the room. At your signal, the first person on each team races to his team's jar and drops in his penny. The coin must go inside the jar before the player can race back to tag the next player in line. Continue until one team finishes.

Play again with the variation of having players walk backward, hop on one foot, skip, and so on.

LESSON 50 SNACK:
Edible Coins

Supplies: Any round treats to represent coins (carrot slices, cucumber slices, banana slices, tortilla chips, round cookies, etc.)

Directions: To remind the children of Matthew's job as a tax collector, serve an assortment of treats that resemble coins.

LESSON 50 PRESCHOOL GAME:
Follow Matthew to Jesus

Supplies: Optional: picture of Jesus or a Bible

Directions: This game is a version of "Follow the Leader." Choose one child to be "Matthew" and lead the way to "Jesus." Designate a spot in your room that Matthew should lead to; you might have a Bible or a picture of Jesus there. All the children line up behind "Matthew" and follow him around the room. They should walk in the same way the leader walks. The leader might hop, turn in a circle, wave arms in the air, or clap hands while marching. When the group has reached "Jesus," choose another "Matthew" and play again.

LESSON 51 SNACK:
Noah's Park Favorites

Supplies: Animal cookies · Gummy worms · Fish crackers · Fruit chunks or any other treat to represent a food that one of your Noah's Park puppets might eat · All of your Noah's Park puppets

Directions: Bring out the Noah's Park puppets (worked by the Park Patrol) to visit with the children during snack time. Let the children try to guess which treat the various puppets like best.

LESSON 51 ELEMENTARY GAME:
Samaritan's Cakewalk

Supplies: Noah's Park CD and CD player · Construction paper in several different colors · Masking tape

Preparation: Use masking tape to tape colored paper in a very large circle on the floor. The circle could lead in a winding path around the room if you have space. This circle represents the road to Jericho that the people in the Bible story walked on.

Directions: Play the Noah's Park CD while children walk on the road. Stop the music at random, and call out a color. Have the children look to see what color paper they are standing on or nearest. Ask the children on the color you called to answer a question. (Sample questions are below.) You could have just one child or let every child on that color answer the question. Then start the music again, and let the kids continue walking on the road to Jericho.

Sample questions: How many people did not stop to help the hurt man in the Bible story? Who did Jesus say is a neighbor? Can you name a "neighbor"? What is today's memory verse? How did the Samaritan help the poor, hurt man? How can you show Jesus' love and care to others?

LESSON 51 SNACK:
Noah's Park Favorites

Supplies: Animal cookies · Gummy worms · Fish crackers · Fruit chunks or any other treat to represent a food that one of your Noah's Park puppets might eat · All of your Noah's Park puppets

Directions: Bring out the Noah's Park puppets (worked by the Park Patrol) to visit with the children during snack time. Let the children try to guess which treat the various puppets like best.

LESSON 51 PRESCHOOL GAME:
Good Samaritan Dash

Supplies: Three different colors of construction paper

Preparation: Cut construction paper into small squares so that you have a square for each child in your class. Use three different colors of paper. Print a "T" on one color of square, an "L" on the second color, and an "S" on the third color.

Directions: Have the children sit in a circle. Place a colored square in front of each child. **There were three men who walked by the hurt man in our story. One was the temple worker. If you have a** (color that has a "T" on it) **square, you are a temple worker in our game. If you have a** (color that has a "L" on it) **square, you are a Levite in our game. If you have a** (color that has a "S" on it) **square, you are a Samaritan in our game.**

Call out a color. All the children with that color stand up and run counterclockwise around the circle and back to their spots. Repeat for all the colors. You could have the children do different actions such as skipping, galloping, walking, and so forth.

LESSON 52 SNACK:
Treat Kabobs

Supplies: Fruit chunks (apples, oranges, canned pineapple, grapes) · Cheese cubes · Mini marshmallows · Toothpicks or short wooden skewers

Directions: Let the children thread the fruit chunks, cheese cubes, and mini marshmallows onto toothpicks or skewers, and then enjoy eating them.

LESSON 52 ELEMENTARY GAME:
Group Shuffle

Supplies: None

Directions: Divide the children into two groups, with one or two children more in one group than the other. The smaller group huddles together, while the slightly larger group holds hands and forms a circle around them. Remind the children that in Bible times, people with leprosy had to stick together and also stay away from others. In this game, the kids in the middle must walk or shuffle to the opposite side of the room, without touching the kids circled around them. The kids in the circle must also move along with the inner group, trying not to touch them. This game is a good exercise in teamwork.

LESSON 52 SNACK:
Treat Kabobs

Supplies: Fruit chunks (apples, oranges, canned pineapple, grapes) · Cheese cubes · Mini marshmallows · Toothpicks or short wooden skewers

Directions: Let the children thread the fruit chunks, cheese cubes, and mini marshmallows onto toothpicks or skewers, and then enjoy eating them.

LESSON 52 PRESCHOOL GAME:
T-H-A-N-K

Supplies: None

Directions: Teach the following words to the song "Bingo."

> **Jesus cares for everyone,**
>
> **And we just want to thank Him!**
>
> **T-H-A-N-K.**
>
> **T-H-A-N-K.**
>
> **T-H-A-N-K.**
>
> **And we just want to thank Him!**

Don't sing the song too quickly so that all can keep up. Once the children know it, let them walk in a circle holding hands while singing. Or you could have them stand still in a circle and clap on the spelled letters as they sing.

LESSON 53 SNACK:
Well of Popcorn

Supplies: Popped popcorn (salted or buttered to taste) · Large bucket or bowl (big enough to hold the popcorn) · Measuring cup with handle · Paper cups or plates

Directions: Let children pretend the popcorn is water in a well. Using the measuring cup as the dipper or bucket, they can dip into the well and scoop out popcorn to pour into their paper cups or plates.

LESSON 53 ELEMENTARY GAME:
Concentration

Supplies: Two sheets of paper per child · Markers

Directions: Explain that for today's game, everyone needs to draw two identical (as much as possible) pictures on two sheets of paper. They should choose a word or picture that relates to today's story or memory verse, such as a well, Jesus, water, a heart, a cross, and so on. Allow the children a minute to draw. Collect the papers and scramble them. Then spread the pictures, drawing-side down, out in rows on the floor or a table.

Children will take turns trying to match pictures. On each turn, a child chooses two pictures and turns them over. If they are identical, the child keeps them. If they're not alike, they're turned back over and the next child tries. Go until all the pictures have been matched. If you have lots of children, break into two groups before mixing up the pictures, and play with smaller groups.

LESSON 53 SNACK:
Well of Popcorn

Supplies: Popped popcorn (salted or buttered to taste) · Large bucket or bowl (big enough to hold the popcorn) · Measuring cup with handle · Paper cups or plates

Directions: Let children pretend the popcorn is water in a well. Using the measuring cup as the dipper or bucket, they can dip into the well and scoop out popcorn to pour into their paper cups or plates.

LESSON 53 PRESCHOOL GAME:
Can You Find My Friend?

Supplies: None

Directions: Have the children sit in a circle. Choose one child to be a helper and stand in the middle of the circle. Say to the helper, **Jesus cares for my friend. Can you find my friend?** Then describe one of the children sitting in the circle without saying his or her name. Once the helper finds the friend, the friend becomes the new helper. Continue playing the game until each child has been "found."